The
Missing Link

- In Theology –

THIRD EDITION
(AMPLIFIED)

Julio A. Rodriguez

The Missing Link
- In Theology -
Copyright © November 2005
Julio A. Rodriguez

ISBN: 978-1-939317-04-9

Original Title: "El Eslabón Perdido – En la Teología"

Translated by Frank Mercado Siuro from original Spanish language.

Published by:

Editorial Nueva Vida, Inc.
53-21 37th Ave., Woodside, NY, 11377

- First edition, published in September 2007
- Second edition, published in July 2009
- Third edition, published in December 2012

Printed in the United States of America

Dedication

To the blessed Holy Spirit, as He has honored me with the special task of communicating these truths, taken me from having nothing and called to His service; for the glory of our Lord Jesus and our heavenly Father.

It has been given to every human being without regard to nationality, tribe, language, or ethnicity, wherever they are on this earth, by the generosity of God we can know the true sense of his grace, freely offered to all humanity through the love of the Lord Jesus Christ and his death on the cross of Calvary.

In love, He sacrificed His life and it was deemed acceptable by the Father, such that we can find peace with God and be justified in His sight, accomplished by His expiatory death; according to the perfect and holy will of our Father.

With love and by His mercy,

Julio Rodriguez

Pr. Julio. A. Rodriguez

"Where sin abounded,
Grace abounded much more"
(Romans 5:20)

My prayer to the Lord is
That all who read this book
Have an open mind
And analyze all the points made
With their Bible, as they are presented,
And may the Spirit of Truth,
The Holy Spirit,
Be their guide in all truth

J.R.

"...And when He had opened the book, He found the place where it was written: "The Spirit of the Lord is upon me, because he has anointed me to preach the gospel to the poor; he has sent me to heal the brokenhearted, to proclaim liberty to the captives and recovery of sight to the blind, to set at liberty those who are oppressed; to proclaim the acceptable year of the lord."

(Lucas 4: 17b-19)

6

CONTENT

Introduction to the Third Edition

As the first edition of the book went to publication in 2007, I became somewhat disquieted knowing the information therein contained would give rise to many questions. The doctrinal content is expansive, but I thought it better to give more information and elaborate on interpreting much of the material that has been debated for some time now.

Back then, I felt of the Lord to publish the book as written and was blessed as He opened up to me the significance of the scripture written by Apostle John:

> *"Having many things to write to you, I did not wish to do so with paper and ink ..."* (2 John 1:12; 3 John 1:13)

On this occasion, the Lord allowed me to increase the amount of applicable verses and write further on key doctrines, which I am sure will lead to greater clarity and understanding of these aspects of biblical truths that have suffered distortion during the course of the long history of the Christian faith.

All who would seek and discover *The Missing Link* that was lost *in* the teaching and application of *Theology*, will be able to experience a more fulfilling life, for the glory of our Lord.

J.R.

Prologue to the First Edition

The time is 11:15 in the morning this last Sunday of June, 2005. We are experiencing the glorious presence of the Lord. The Lord encourages us with a Word from Isaiah 60.

It reads:

> *"Arise, shine; For your light has come! And the glory of the LORD is risen upon you. For behold, the darkness shall cover the earth, And deep darkness the people; But the LORD will arise over you, And His glory will be seen upon you. The Gentiles shall come to your light, And kings to the brightness of your rising."* (Isaiah 60: 1-3)

As the service continues, our assistant pastor for youth is scheduled to preach. The people are enjoying the move of the Holy Spirit in a special manner. Our inner ear is attentive and we sense a receptive attitude. Suddenly our speaker cites a biblical passage found in the book of Esther:

> *"For if you remain completely silent at this time, relief and deliverance will arise for the Jews from another place, but you and your father's house will perish. Yet who knows whether you have come to the kingdom for such a time as this?* (Esther 4:14)

At this time the message becomes a personal conversation with the Holy Spirit who brings to remembrance the many ways He had been speaking to me.

I am compelled to write on this theme, though truthfully, I'd rather not. It's very conflictive. I identify with Moses when God instructed him to return to Egypt and present himself before Pharaoh.

I question, **"Why me, Lord?"** You have great and influential preachers and servants; world renowned. Why can't you send one of them to at least begin the message, and then I can join them?

The Lord is patient and merciful and doesn't become angry with me; but instead gives me some reasons in answer to my questions.

To begin with, I'm reminded that: *"If a grain of wheat goes not into the ground and dies, it remains alone, but if it dies, it then bears much fruit."* The word **"dies"** is what causes my anguish.

I had believed I left all to serve Him and in a manner of speaking, died to my ego and personal desires, but the Lord indicates there is still an area He expects me to give up: the assurance of my ministry. The love I felt when received and accepted.

He expects me to surrender my expectations and only wait on Him as His plan for these crucial times unfolds. Part of Queen Esther's response was:

> *"...And so I will go to the king, which is against the law; and if I perish, I perish!"* (Ester 4:16)

I still hear the preacher's voice: "This is the time, the *"Kairos"* of God". **This is the time!**

J.R.

This is the situation:

It has been many years since the Holy Spirit stirs within me and directs me into an analysis of Scripture that is unconventional; that does not coincide with what I usually hear and ponder from anointed people used by God with signs and wonders around the world.

The Lord has shown me a new form of "**Tradition**" that has supplanted the truth. It is a tradition so deeply rooted that it's difficult to speak or think on it without accepting it as truth.

It's a tradition that is surely the result of a powerful satanic strategy that has affected and discredited Christianity to such a degree of diminished credibility in our faith for a lost and needy world.

This tradition has such a radical perspective on human salvation that we lose all concerning the fear of God, and His dealings with mankind.

Theological questions need us to answer.

1. What happens to a person that dies without receiving the Lord Jesus Christ as his personal Savior, if no one ever spoke to them of Christ? Is there a remote possibility that God allows him to enter heaven?

2. What happens to people with faith in Jesus, who continue religious rituals that are an abomination to God, but nevertheless live in sincere faith with Christian love, in the hope the Lord will receive them in heaven on that day?

3. What shall happen to those who claim to be Christians, but their testimonies demonstrate otherwise? Will they enter heaven in spite of this?

It would seem obvious to state: This is a thorny and controversial subject. The easy path would be to accept what we have heard, and that which tradition may have taught us, not withstanding, the Lord persists and tells me:

It's time for **ALL** the truth. **Now is the time!**

Two weeks ago the Lord challenged me, He asked me:

> *Are you willing to risk your reputation in proclamation of the truth?*

He reminded me during the time of ministry we consider Christ Jesus was "popular", He always told the truth (though it may have been unpopular). Consequentially, on many occasions He was threatened with violence.

My answer, after momentary reflection, was an unconditional yes; though I could imagine the attitude and severe criticism of some who could not comprehend.

For a long time I've waited for others to enter a discourse on this theme, be it a local, national, or international figure. I diligently searched the internet to see if someone had taken the initiative to discuss this topic, but as of today there has been no answer.

I've consulted and researched many books and seen that this theme is ignored. The many Bible commentaries have excluded this and no one has dared to confront this Christian tradition.

The Lord would say:

> *"unless a grain of wheat falls into the ground and dies, it remains alone; but if it dies, it produces much grain."*
> (John 12:24)

The Holy Spirit would reveal to me that, although in my ministry I've always attempted to work with a team and seek advice in all I felt necessary; I had to go it alone in what he was now asking.

In remembering our Lord Jesus Christ, He was alone as He obeyed and went to the cross. No one was able to share this with Him; Apostles nor followers, not even his own mother was able.

The Lord has asked me to sacrifice my "Isaac" and expects my obedience, as did Abraham, though I do not understand God's motive for this request.

In my indecision the Lord reminds me that He'll always be with me, and that he'll never abandon me in any time of persecution.

Though I walk through the fire, He will provide all the protection I need to keep me whole.

But... the Lord inquires of us all:

Who else is there willing to give up great popularity in their sphere of influence within Christianity and suffer persecution, for the cause of truth?

MAKING THE TRUTH FIT:

Accommodating a new tradition

MAKING THE TRUTH FIT: Accommodating a new tradition

The Bible says:

> *"A son honors his father, and a servant his master. If then I am a father, where is my honor? And if I am a master, **where is my fear?** says the LORD of hosts to you..."* (Malachi 1:6. ESV)

> *"Whoever walks in uprightness **fears the LORD**, but he who is devious in his ways despises him"* (Prov. 14:2)[i]

> *"The **fear of the LORD** is the beginning of wisdom"* (Prov. 9:10)

> *"The **reward** for humility and **fear of the LORD** is riches and honor and life."* (Prov. 22:4)

The Gospel of Mark relates how Jesus confronted the Jews and religious people of his time, condemning the rituals they had established as valid before God's eyes.

He said:

> *"Well did Isaiah prophesy of you hypocrites, as it is written, "'This people honors me with their lips, but their heart is far from me; in vain do they worship me, teaching as doctrines the commandments of men.' You leave the commandment of God and hold to the tradition of men.*

> *"...thus making void the word of God by your tradition that you have handed down..."* (Mark 7: 6-8; 13[a])

The Lord has revealed to me that this new "**tradition**" that has been accepted in these last generations are **thoughts and**

doctrinal ideas that substituted the veracity of the message of God given in His Word.

We should not be surprised that Christianity has largely lost its powerful influence in the world (to the degree it's considered we now live in the "Post- Christian Era").

Much of the expression of dogma that form the body of Christian thought as it evolved through centuries; provoked a falling away of faith in the majority, and a sense of frustration in many others.

One strain of thought is the following:

> *"There are two forms of interpreting the Bible and both, though they are contradictory, will agree in meaning and the essence of what is written".*

This is similar to humanistic relativism:

> *"The truth is relative and depends on the interpretation you attribute to it".*

This expression is usually used by those attempting to understand either the Calvinist or the Arminian viewpoints, which we shall further elaborate on.

A brief description of the 5 premises of Calvinism and the 5 of Arminianism

FIRST POINT

CALVINIST:
TOTAL DEPRIVATION or TOTAL INABILITY

Due to the fall, man is incapable of believing in the gospel of salvation on his own. A sinner is deaf, blind, and dead to the things of God. His heart is deceitful and desperately wicked.

He hasn't a free will and is enslaved by his evil nature; subsequently, he is not able to choose for good over evil in a spiritual sense.

As a consequence, more than the insistence of the Holy Spirit is required for a sinner to come to Christ. Regeneration is necessary, by which the Holy Spirit gives life and a new nature. Faith is not man's contribution to his salvation; but is rather part of this same gift of salvation.

ARMINIAN·
HUMAN CAPACITY, SELF WILL or FREE WILL

Although man's will was seriously compromised by the fall, his natural state has not been left in total spiritual abandonment. God graciously enables every sinner with the capacity to repent and believe, without any interference in the choice a man makes. Every sinner possesses free will and their eternal destiny is determined by this use of choice.

The freedom mankind enjoys consists in our ability to choose for good over bad, in spiritual matters. Our will is not enslaved by our sinful nature. Every sinner has the power to cooperate with the Holy Spirit and be regenerated, or resist the grace of God and perish.

The lost person needs the assistance of the Holy Spirit, but does not have to be regenerated before he is able to believe; leaving the Holy Spirit to begin His work of regeneration, progressing and perfecting by sanctification after a sinner surrenders his life to God.

A person contributes faith to his salvation.

SECOND POINT

CALVINIST:
UNCONDITIONAL ELECTION

The selection by God of certain individuals for salvation, before the foundation of the world, rested only on His own sovereign will.

This selection of any particular sinners was not based on the foreknowledge of the response or obedience of an individual, but on the contrary, God gives the faith and repentance to each person he has elected.

Their responses are the result, not the reason, of God's election. Therefore the election was not determined nor had a condition of any virtuous quality or action foresaw by God in any man. God enables all those chosen by his sovereign will, to accept Christ by the power of the Holy Spirit.

ARMINIAN:
CONDITIONAL ELECTION

The election God has made of certain individuals for salvation, before the foundation of the world, has been based on the foreknowledge of God, in that He knows what their response to the call of salvation will be.

God has chosen only those whom He knew would freely choose to believe the gospel and receive Christ. This election is determined and conditional on an action. Therefore the act of deciding to believe in Christ, rather than God's selection of a particular sinner, is the ultimate reason for salvation.

THIRD POINT

CALVINIST:
LIMITED ATONEMENT OR PARTIAL REDEMPTION

The work of redemption completed by Christ had the intention of saving only those persons God had elected to save, and consequently assure the salvation of these elected ones.

The atoning death of Christ then only pays the price for the sin of those sinners elected.

In addition to forgetting their sins, Christ's redemption provided everything for their salvation, including the faith that would unite them with Him.

The gift of faith is perfectly applied by the Holy Spirit to all the elect Christ died for, and the finished work guarantees their salvation.

ARMINIAN:
GENERAL ATONEMENT OR UNIVERSAL REDEMPTION

The work of redemption by Christ has made it possible for all mankind to be saved, but has no guarantee for any one particular person. Although Christ died for all and everyone can be saved, only those who believe in Him are saved.

His death has allowed God to forgive the sins of anyone, with the condition of faith in Christ. Redemption through Christ is applied only when a person accepts this salvation.

FOURTH POINT

CALVINIST:
IRRESISTIBLE GRACE OR THE CALL OF THE HOLY SPIRIT

In addition to the general call to salvation made to all those who hear the gospel, the Holy Spirit extends an inner special call to the elect, and inevitably saves them. The general call (which is made to call men without preference) can be rejected, but the particular call (which is only for the elect) cannot be rejected and always leads to conversion.

In this particular call the Holy Spirit brings sinners to Christ in an irresistible manner. The Holy Spirit is not limited by human volition neither depends on any cooperation by man to accomplish the work of salvation in mankind.

The Holy Spirit graciously obliges those elect sinners to cooperate, believe, and repent, in liberty and willingly to Christ. The grace of God is invincible. It never fails to save those whom it has been offered by God.

ARMINIAN:
THE HOLY SPIRIT CAN BE RESISTED

The Holy Spirit makes an inner call to all those who hear the invitation of the gospel; but since each person has free will; it is possible to reject the Holy Spirit and this call.

Regeneration cannot occur by the Holy Spirit until there is faith. Faith (which is man's contribution) precedes and makes possible the new birth.

Therefore, the free will of man can limit the ability of the Holy Spirit to apply the finished work of Christ. He can only rescue those who allow him. When a response is not adequate, the Holy Spirit can give no life to a sinner. In conclusion, God's grace is not invincible. It can be, and frequently is, resisted and frustrated by man.

FIFTH POINT:

CALVINIST:
THE SAINTS WILL PERSEVERE

All those elected by God, redeemed by Christ and that have accepted the faith given them by the Holy Spirit, are eternally secure in their salvation. The power of God sustains their faith and they all persevere until the end.

ARMINIAN:
ONE CAN FALL FROM GRACE

All those who have believed and been saved, can lose their salvation if they do not retain their faith in Christ and persevere until the end.

Religious Relativism

Religious Relativism

As we can appreciate, the discussion of the offer of salvation in Christ, unfortunately, has been framed within the context of two polarizing positions: **Limited atonement versus unlimited atonement.**

Typically, those in favor of one or the other theological current focus on the portions of scripture they deem favorable to their position. We are surprised as we see how secular relativism has infiltrated Christianity, and considering morality does not exist in relativism, it states *"nothing is correct or incorrect but all depends on the lens from which it is seen."*

It's as if to say a belief in something that does not offend your conscience is correct for you, though it may be another person has a diametrically opposed opinion as yours, but if they believe and their conscience accuses them not, they're also correct.

This way of thinking is not right; as it is clear there is only one truth, impregnable and indestructible; and there should be no confusion as to it. Jesus Christ is the truth and He alone can reveal the mysteries of this life. We are 100% sure that God has revealed this to all humanity.

The Bible declares:

> *"The secret things belong to the LORD our God, but the things that are revealed belong to us and to our children forever, that we may do all the words of this law"* (Deuteronomy 29:29)

And also:

> *"My people are destroyed for lack of knowledge" (Hosea 4:6)*

In a manner of speaking, those whose background has been grounded in Calvinist thought believe they form part of an elect group chosen by God and it matters not what they do or don't do, heaven is certain for them; and in contrast, those taught the Arminian current believe heaven is not assured to anyone as it depends on one maintaining himself in holiness and not fall (habitual sin).

When someone comes to the foot of the cross and receives salvation through grace, that person is normally instructed in a church and in a short time begins to reflect on their actions, manner of speech, etc., and the stream of thought in the "indoctrination" to Christianity.

When our everyday citizen analyzes his existence and begins to question what his destiny will be after he leaves this world, they normally seek answers in religion and sooner or later are submerged in the sea of contradictory opinions and beliefs. The discovery of the multitude of religions and sects will leave them uncertain as to who actually knows and practices the truth (and sometimes will question if absolute truth really exists).

Normally, in the Christian world we speak of Christ and his work of redemption; but we are constantly accusing each other (as it depends in the manner we comprehend or have been taught the Scriptures); and instead of an example of love to this world, unity and peace, we confuse those coming to our churches for answers.

Although we preach Jesus, we do not live by the words of Jesus. We can recall the question of the Lord on one occasion:

"Why do you call me 'Lord, Lord,' and not do what I tell you?
(Luke 6: 46)

WHAT SHALL WE DO?

First and fundamentally, let us return to the Word. We should recognize we are not walking as God would have us and make the necessary adjustments.

What were we told and believed that the Word of God does not prove? Was our belief based on the influence of someone important, or learned?

Are we faithful or not, to the integrity of the Word of God?

Let us recall the words of the Apostle Paul:

> *"The natural person does not accept the things of the Spirit of God, for they are folly to him, and he is not able to understand them because they are spiritually discerned. The spiritual person judges all things, but is himself to be judged by no one."*
> (1 Corinthians 2: 14-15)

We should be very cautious in our Bible study and note the importance of seeking **scriptural equilibrium** of God in any doctrine.

This will help us avoid all extremes that inadvertently frustrate believers instead of edifying, as we walk with the Lord.

Let us learn to see the Bible AS A WHOLE and not dwell solely on a small portion (especially when a truth is not that crystal clear or is ambiguous).

God desires that we come to the knowledge of all the truth.

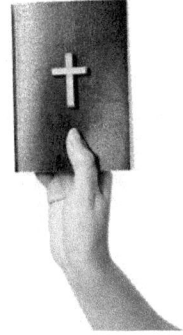

King David said:

> *"Come, O children, listen to me; I will teach **you the fear of the LORD.** What man is there who desires life and loves many days, that he may see good? Keep your tongue from evil and your lips from speaking deceit. Turn away from evil and do good; seek peace and pursue it."* (Psalm 34: 11-14)

The Lord has made known to me that in what the world labels "post-Christian era", He calls this the:

"ERA of CHRISTIAN RENOVATION"

Allowing us to understand there are glorious times ahead for the church of God on this earth.

Pray to our Lord that we all may participate in this move of God over all the face of the earth

A KEY WORD

In the gospel of John we find a word that may greatly illuminate our understanding.

Jesus said:

> "I am the way, the truth, and the life: no man cometh unto the Father, but **BY** me." (John 14:6. KJV)

The key word we wish to analyze is '**BY**' (Gr. "*dia*")

This word has <u>two meanings</u>.
On the one hand it means "across" or "*through*", and another meaning is *"because of"* or "as a result of what has been done."

We will verify that **both meanings** are valid in the redemptory work of Jesus

Normally we accept only the **first meaning** as correct.

Traditionally we understand that Jesus said *"no one comes to the Father* except *'through' me"*

The validity of this first interpretation leads to our inquiries regarding the provision made by God for those who reside in a remote corner of our planet, and have not heard of Christ.

They live a "normal" life depending on the mores of the culture in their native land; nevertheless, *how can they go to heaven if they die without anyone speaking to them of Christ?*

Let us take notice that if we analyze this verse and accept the **second meaning** of the word "by", we may give it the significance: *"no one can come to the Father if not **"because"** of me"*.

In other words Jesus lets us know that had He not completed the work of redemption successfully, mankind would never have been able to enter heaven.

Not even King David or Abraham would enter.

Jesus stated at that time that the just souls waited in **"Abraham's Bosom"** (Luke 16:22) and were not risen to heaven until Jesus conquered Satan and restored all things.

ANALYSIS OF WHAT OCCURRED

ADAM	CHRIST
He did not exist (Genesis2:5)	Eternally existed (John 1:1)
Was made of dust (Gen. 2:7) And was given dominion (Gen. 1:28; 2:19)	Existing in the form of God, counted not the being on an equality with God a thing to be grasped, but emptied himself, taking the form of a servant, being made in the likeness of men (Philip. 2: 6-8. ASV)
Lived in paradise, without strife, without attacks (Gen. 2: 15-16)	Lived in dangerous times; suffered persecution and violence (from the time he entered his mother's womb there were threats of death)
with all this allowed himself to be overcome by the evil one and disobeyed.	In all, He was obedient unto the hour of death, death on a cross.
In the middle of the abundance, he lost everything (Gen. 3: 23-24)	In the scornful death of the cross He gained redemption of all Adam had lost; defeating Satan and evil forces. (Col. 2:15)

The Word also tells us that during the time the body of Jesus lay in the tomb, the Lord **"went and preached to all those souls in chains"** (1 Peter 3:19);

And Ephesians 4 declares:

> *"Therefore He says: "when He ascended on high, He led captivity captive, and gave gifts to men..."*   (Ephesians 4: 8-10)

Those who died with the hope that God is faithful to His promise are no longer in Abraham's Bosom; **Jesus brought them to heaven!**

We are also told that Jesus, in his overcoming and completed work:

> *"**God also has highly exalted Him and given Him the name which is above every name,** that at the name of Jesus every knee should bow, of those in heaven, and of those on earth, and of those under the earth, and that every tongue should confess that Jesus Christ is Lord, to the glory of God the Father"*   (Philippians 2: 9-11)

> *"...who (Jesus) has gone into heaven and is at the right hand of God, **angels and authorities and powers having been made subject to Him.**"*   (1 Peter 3:22)

> *"But one of the elders said to me, "Do not weep. Behold, the Lion of the tribe of Judah, the Root of David, **has prevailed** to open the scroll and to loose its seven seals ..."*

> *"...And every creature which is in heaven and on the earth and under the earth and such as are in the sea, and all that are in them, I heard saying: "Blessing and honor and glory and power Be **to Him who sits on the throne, And to the Lamb,** forever and ever!" Then the four living creatures said, "Amen!";*

> *"And the twenty-four elders fell down and worshiped Him who lives forever and ever."*   (Revelation 5: 5-14)

We read a verse in the Bible that reveals a great truth and we understand **there was also something that would occur in heaven that would have to reconciled**, and was fulfilled with the death of Jesus on the cross.

It states:

> *"...and by Him to reconcile all things to Himself, by Him, whether things on earth or things in heaven, having made peace through the blood of His cross. "*   (Colossians 1:20)

WHAT WAS THIS?

The Bible declares there was once a rebellion in heaven and the protagonist was none other than Satan, who was a cherubim, *"perfect in all his ways from the day he was created, until sin was found in him." (Ezekiel 14:28-29)* and he was cast out of heaven.

Isaiah says the following:

> *"Yet you shall be brought down to Sheol, To the lowest depths of the Pit. "* (Isaiah 14:15)

Following are the passages that speak of this event, in **Ezekiel 28** and **Isaiah 14**:

Ezekiel 28: 12b – 19

> *"'Thus says the Lord GOD: "You were the seal of perfection, Full of wisdom and perfect in beauty. You were in Eden, the garden of God; Every precious stone was your covering: The sardius, topaz, and diamond, Beryl, onyx, and jasper, Sapphire, turquoise, and emerald with gold. The workmanship of your timbrels and pipes Was prepared for you on the day you were created.*
>
> *"You were the anointed cherub who covers; I established you; You were on the holy mountain of God; You walked back and forth in the midst of fiery stones.*

You were perfect in your ways from the day you were created, Till iniquity was found in you.

"By the abundance of your trading You became filled with violence within, And you sinned; Therefore I cast you as a profane thing Out of the mountain of God; And I destroyed you, O covering cherub, From the midst of the fiery stones.

"Your heart was lifted up because of your beauty; You corrupted your wisdom for the sake of your splendor; I cast you to the ground, I laid you before kings, That they might gaze at you.
"You defiled your sanctuaries By the multitude of your iniquities, By the iniquity of your trading; Therefore I brought fire from your midst; It devoured you, And I turned you to ashes upon the earth In the sight of all who saw you.

All who knew you among the peoples are astonished at you; You have become a horror, And shall be no more forever." ' "

Isaiah 14: 12-15

"How you are fallen from heaven, O Lucifer, son of the morning! How you are cut down to the ground, You who weakened the nations!
For you have said in your heart: 'I will ascend into heaven, I will exalt my throne above the stars of God; I will also sit on the mount of the congregation On the farthest sides of the north; I will ascend above the heights of the clouds, I will be like the Most High.'
Yet you shall be brought down to Sheol, To the lowest depths of the Pit."

When Jesus died on the cross, there was great peace in heaven. The consequence of God's judgment against Lucifer may have appeared unjust or too severe

We now know that God is perfect in His judgments.

Jesus demonstrates it was possible to obey God always, even in our most terrible moments..

Jesus, with perfect obedience, restored the true significance of God's justice.

Lucifer rebelled and disobeyed.

Jesus always obeyed and conquered.

OBEDIENCE BRINGS: ***VICTORY AND PEACE!***

BELIEVE, CONFIDE and OBEY should be impressionable words in our life.

In the following chapter we will analyze a central doctrine that attempts to explain why human beings disobey and commit sin.

A Doctrine that has influenced history:

"ORIGINAL SIN"

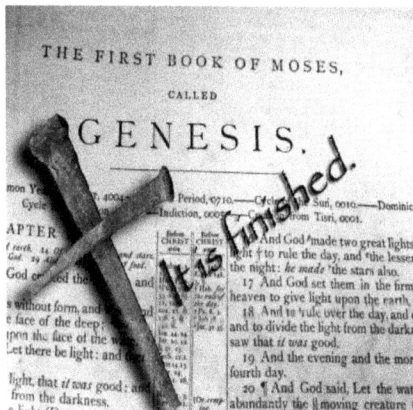

A Doctrine that has influenced history: "ORIGINAL SIN"

We shall proceed to analyze **a doctrine that has caused great confusion** within the Christian world, and furthermore, many souls have not come to Christ and received the grace of God because of this foundational premise in theology.

We shall speak of what has been accepted as the *"Doctrine of Original Sin"* in Christianity.

THIS DOCTRINE HAS BEEN TAUGHT THE FOLLOWING WAY:

<< Original Sin. This includes our guilt and inherent sin. Adam sinned, and it was imputed to us. As our representative he sinned, making us also guilty of sin. As a consequence we have inherited the tendency to sin and are predisposed to its commission. Man became totally depraved by nature>>[ii]

<< We believe by the disobedience of Adam original sin affected all humanity, and all nature is corrupted. Sin is a sickness that is hereditary and ultimately includes every fetus in the uterus of its mother, produces all manner of rebellion in man, at the very core; being as a result a vile and repugnant abomination in the sight of God it is then sufficient reason to condemn all humanity >>[iii]

<< It is also taught that since the fall of Adam all men have been conceived in sin and are born with the sin nature as a matter of course. This is to say, all lust and are inclined to evil from the time of birth, incapable of knowing the fear of God and true faith in God. Furthermore, our innate sickness caused by hereditary sin is of a reality the sin and condemnation that brings the wrath of God on all those not born again through immersion in the baptismal waters, and born of the Holy Spirit. >>[iv]

The Bible teaches us in the book of Romans:

*"Therefore, just as **through one man sin entered the world**, and death through sin, and thus death spread to all men, because all sinned—".*

*"For if by the one man's offense death reigned through the one, much more those who receive abundance of grace and of the gift of righteousness **will reign in life through the One, Jesus Christ.)**"*

*"Therefore, as through one man's offense judgment came to all men, resulting in condemnation, even **so through one Man's righteous act the free gift came to all men**, resulting in justification of life."*

"For as by one man's disobedience many were made sinners, so also by one Man's obedience many will be made righteous."
(Romans 5: 12, 17-19)

It is interesting to note that **within the same chapter** that the principal sense of the doctrine of original sin is found (v.12), the Bible states that on the merit of Christ, the justification for life is available to all mankind (v.18), as long as grace and forgiveness are chosen.

"And the Spirit and the bride say, "Come!" And let him who hears say, "Come!" And let him who thirsts come. Whoever desires, let him take the water of life freely."
(Revelation 22:17)

Those who teach the doctrine of the original sin give to understand (perhaps without knowing it), that the **sin** of Adam <u>is more powerful</u> that the **triumph** of Christ

We have been taught that by the sin of Adam the human race was contaminated, and we are born with this blemish of sin. Nevertheless, the Bible declares that **Jesus removed all the effects of sin** that weighed on humanity through Adam.

> *"Christ has redeemed us from the curse of the law, having become a curse for us (for it is written, "cursed is everyone who hangs on a tree")"* (Gal. 3:13)

The Word also says:

> *"And you, being dead in your trespasses and the uncircumcision of your flesh, **He has made alive** together with Him, having forgiven you all trespasses, having **wiped out** the handwriting of requirements that was against us, which was contrary to us. And He has taken it out of the way, having nailed it to the cross.*
> *Having disarmed principalities and powers, He made a public spectacle of them, triumphing over them in it. "* (Col. 2: 13-15)

43

How did it all begin?

Let us examine a period of history, as reliable sources recount:

<< "It was universally believed that man was created in the image of God, pure and holy, and the fall was his own fault. The magnitude of man's sin and the dire consequences were not fully debated before the controversy between Pelagius and Augustine in the Fifth century." >> [v]

<< Throughout man's history, the theology of depravity has been attributed to Adam. Augustine, (354-430 AD) who is credited with the concept of original sin, submitted that the fall of Adam corrupted mankind, transforming the human race into a mass of sin. All men inherit both traits: the pull of sin and the guilt, because in Adam's sin all humanity has sinned." >>[vi]

<< Pelagius (370-440 AD) rejecting the argument of those that insisted human frailty was the reason for their sin, made the point that God created all human beings free to choose between good and bad; and sin is a voluntary choice. Celestius, a disciple of Pelagius, rejected the church doctrine of original sin and the necessity of infant baptism.

He (Pelagius) blamed the moral laxity in Rome for the doctrine of "divine grace" (as taught by Augustine). He attacked this teaching in all the territories where moral law was in jeopardy. He reasoned that if one were not responsible for his good or bad actions, no one would refrain themselves from indulging in sin. Pelagius soon had a considerable amount of followers in Rome." >> [vii]

<< Calvin instructed with precision the correct concept of man before the fall: "Man possessed the freedom and the will to desire and fulfill that which is good and pleasing to God in his former state of innocence." "God ordained that the nature of man had freedom and power to act upon and bring about whatever he chose, so that man was not forced nor compelled through his nature to commit either good or evil." >>[viii]

When we ANALYZE the Scriptures, we discover:

Adam and Eve were created in a state of innocence and **were good** *(Gen.1:27, 31)*

The Word of God teaches us that there is a time in a person's life, when they have no understanding and cannot discern between good and evil *(Deut. 1:39)* and they **cannot reject evil and choose good** *(Isaiah 7:15-16)*

When sin is committed there is a separation between God and the person who chose to sin *(Isaiah 59:1-2)*

God has made clear that the spiritual consequences that sin brings fall completely on the person committing the act of sin. He says: *"The soul who sins shall die"* *(Ezekiel 18: 2-4, 20)*

God will judge each one according to the harsh words they have spoken and their individual actions (Matthew 12:36-37; Romans 2:6; 2 Corinthians 5:10; Revelation 20: 12-15)

- Jesus Christ paid the price required by God to remove the sin of Adam (Romans 5: 15-21; Hebrews 9)
- He is the second Adam (1 Corinthians 15:45-49) who came from heaven to restore what the first Adam had lost (Matthew 18:11);
- And He redeemed us from the curse (Galatians 3:13)

Jesus used the children as an example of humility (Matthew 18: 2-4) Jesus also said the kingdom of heaven is made up of children (Mark 10: 14-15)

The Apostle Paul used children as a model of purity
(1 Corinthians 14:20)

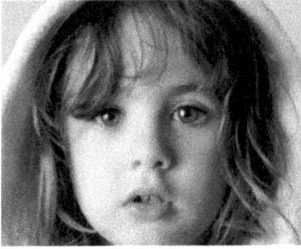

It is a fact that neither Jesus nor the first Christians believed or taught that newborn babies entered this world already sinners but this same doctrine was introduced in the **fifth century** of this era;

Therefore, we should believe and understand that the preceding Biblical verses **are showing us**:

- "The whole human race **is born** in a state of **innocence**, the same as Adam in the garden of Eden (signifying that **no child is destined for hell, but goes to heaven**); and

- When someone, after being able to discern good and evil, exercising their free will decides to disobey God and is corrupted, suffers a spiritual death until they repent and receive, also voluntarily, grace for forgiveness and are justified by God through Jesus Christ.

The Case of King David

The Case of King David

In reading Psalm 51, we may be **predisposed** to believe that David sinned before being born (or conceived); but as we further examine the circumstance he speaks directly of, a more perfect understanding is achieved.

David said:

> *"Behold, I was shapen in iniquity; and in sin did my mother conceive me."* (Psalm 51:5)

David was referring to what transpired in his mother's life.

LET US EXAMINE THOSE VERSES:

1 Chronicles 2: 13-17

> *"**Jesse begot** Eliab his firstborn, Abinadab the second, Shimea the third, Nethanel the fourth, Raddai the fifth, Ozem the sixth, and **David** the seventh. Now **their sisters were Zeruiah and Abigail**. And the sons of Zeruiah were Abishai, Joab, and Asahel—three.*
> *Abigail bore Amasa; and the father of Amasa was Jether the Ishmaelite."*

2° Samuel 17:25

> *"And Absalom made Amasa captain of the army instead of Joab. This Amasa was the son of a man whose name was Jithra, an Israelite, who had gone in to **Abigail the <u>daughter of Nahash</u>, sister of Zeruiah**, Joab's mother."*

1° Samuel 12:12

> *"And when you saw that **Nahash** king of the Ammonites came against you, you said to me, 'No, but a king shall reign over us,' when the LORD your God was your king."*

In these verses, the Bible narrative speaks of the two daughters of the ammonite King **Nahash**, named **Abigail** and **Zeruiah**; and we also find they were David's sisters (now David's father was Jesse, not Nahash).

We understand by this that David's mother was the wife of King Nahash and **had committed adultery** with Jesse. *The fruit of this relationship was David.*

This brings light and explains the reason Jesse did not wish to present David to Samuel (1 Samuel 16: 1-13), when he went to Jesse's household to anoint one of his children as the future king of Israel:

> *"Thus Jesse made seven of his sons pass before Samuel. And Samuel said to Jesse, "The LORD has not chosen these." And Samuel said to Jesse, "Are all the young men here?" Then he said, "There remains yet the youngest, and there he is, keeping the sheep."*
> *And Samuel said to Jesse, "Send and bring him. For we will not sit down till he comes here." So he sent and brought him in. Now he was ruddy, with bright eyes, and good-looking. And the LORD said, "Arise, anoint him; for this is the one!"*
>
> *Then Samuel took the horn of oil and anointed him in the midst of his brothers; and the Spirit of the LORD came upon David from that day forward. So Samuel arose and went to Ramah."*
> (1 Samuel 16:10-13)

We can also see with clarity why David's brothers had so little esteem for him:

> *"Now David was the son of that Ephrathite of Bethlehem Judah, whose name was Jesse, and who had eight sons. And the man was old, advanced in years, in the days of Saul.*
>
> *The three oldest sons of Jesse had gone to follow Saul to the battle. The names of his three sons who went to the battle were Eliab the firstborn, next to him Abinadab, and the third*

Shammah. David was the youngest. And the three oldest followed Saul. (1 Samuel 17: 12-14)

"Now Eliab his oldest brother heard when he spoke to the men; and Eliab's anger was aroused against David, and he said, "Why did you come down here? And with whom have you left those few sheep in the wilderness? I know your pride and the insolence of your heart, for you have come down to see the battle."
(1 Samuel 17:28).

We can better understand why David did not name any of his brothers as military leaders in his army, but he chose the children of his sisters;

In addition we see the reason King Nahash held a special appreciation for David and *"shown him mercy"*.

The Bible tells us when David fled from Absalom, King Nahash sent his son Shobi to show him mercy during this difficult period he had to pass through.

The Holy Scriptures give us this narrative:

"So Israel and Absalom encamped in the land of Gilead. Now it happened, when David had come to Mahanaim, that Shobi the son of Nahash from Rabbah of the people of Ammon, Machir the son of Ammiel from Lo Debar, and Barzillai the Gileadite from Rogelim, brought beds and basins, earthen vessels and wheat, barley and flour, parched grain and beans, lentils and parched seeds, honey and curds, sheep and cheese of the herd, for David and the people who were with him to eat. For they said, "The people are hungry and weary and thirsty in the wilderness." (2 Samuel 17: 26-29)

It happened after this that Nahash the king of the people of Ammon died, and his son reigned in his place. Then David said, "I will show kindness to Hanun the son of Nahash, because his father showed kindness to me." So David sent messengers to comfort him concerning his father. And David's servants came to Hanun in the land of the people of Ammon to comfort him".
(1 Chronicles 19: 1-2)

51

SOMETHING MORE,

The Bible tells us that David did not choose any of his brothers to occupy positions of importance by his side in the king's palace. Nevertheless, he did not withhold his mercy from any of them and placed them in charge of *"every matter pertaining to God and the business of the king",* rulers over the tribe of Reuben and the Gadites (1 Chronicles 26: 32)

The last detail we will examine in the story of King David as we read in 1 Chron. 2:13-17 the names of six of David's brothers. They are [Eliab, and Abinadab, Shimma *(mentioned 'Shammah' in 1 Samuel 17:13)* Nethaneel, Raddai, Ozem];

And 1 Samuel 17:12 tells us that Jesse had **eight** sons. Then,

Who was the eighth son of Jesse?

In the first book of Chronicles we are told of **Elihu** of Judah, "one of the brothers of David"… (1 Chron. 27:18).

This was the only brother David gave a position to within the circle of officials close to the king:

> *"And the children of Israel, according to their number, the heads of fathers' houses, the captains of thousands and hundreds and their officers, served the king in every matter of the military divisions. These divisions came in and went out month by month throughout all the months of the year...* (1 Chron. 27:1)

The Lord Jesus tells us:

"Search the Scriptures" *(John 5:39)*

This is precisely what we endeavor to do as we continue to expound in the following pages.

The relationship between the Omniscience of God and the will of those created

The relationship between the Omniscience of God and the will of those created

There are many people unfamiliar with God who cannot understand Him, and they are puzzled by the disconnect they perceive in the history of man from the time of his creation to our present day. They have questions that need answers.

They know God is eternal and omnipotent:

> *"Indeed before the day was, I am He; And there is no one who can deliver out of My hand; I work, and who will reverse it?"* (Isaiah 43:13)

> *"...*Is there a God besides Me? Indeed *there is* no other Rock; I know not *one.'"* (Isaiah 44:8)

> *"'Ah, Lord GOD! Behold, You have made the heavens and the earth by Your great power and outstretched arm. There is nothing too hard for You"* (Jeremiah 32:17)

We read in the Bible that God is also omniscient; he searches hearts and knows our thoughts and our intentions. All humanity is exposed to Him at once. (Jeremiah 17:10);

The Bible says there is not a word we will utter He is not aware of beforehand. (Psalm 139:4);

He knows the spiritual state of every person and what each needs to walk the narrow road to salvation. He knows of everything that exists on earth (Job 38, 39, 40, 41); all knowledge of our vast solar system, our galaxy, and the billions of galaxies He created. Nothing escapes His gaze and wisdom!
...

Some disturbing questions

Since God knows everything, has all power, is great in mercy and grace, and His Word clearly lets us know He does not take pleasure in the death of a sinner, but wishes him to live:

[For I have no pleasure in the death of one who dies," says the Lord GOD. "Therefore turn and live!" (Ezekiel 18:32)]

Then,

> - Why doesn't He act with more intensity to reach those who are lost, in this manner not having to condemn them to eternal punishment?

If God knew beforehand that Satan would wreck such havoc on the creation formed by Him, then:

- Why did He create Satan?
- Why did He give allow Satan the capacity to become proud?
- Why didn't He make him unable to commit sin?

When He cast Satan down from his position in heaven:

- Why did He banish him to earth and not another place in the universe?

On the other hand, if Satan had to be sent to earth;

- Couldn't God have created man stronger than Satan?
- Why didn't He choose to create Adam and Eve incapable of disobeying Him?

If Satan would not have had access to the garden while Adam and Eve were there, sin would never have been introduced on earth and the human race would continue clean and pure in the presence of its Creator. We never would have to worry about confronting a rebellious spiritual being.

Furthermore, without the prohibition given to them, Satan would not have had any way to tempt mankind; and consequently they could not have fallen into disobedience.

Following up on this thought:

- What was the reason Adam and Eve were not allowed to eat of the fruit of one of the trees in the Garden of Eden?
  …

… There are so many questions similar to these that can be presented.

The apostle Paul, in meditating on questions concerning the sovereign God said:

" As it is written, "JACOB I HAVE LOVED, BUT ESAU I HAVE HATED." What shall we say then? Is there unrighteousness with God? Certainly not!

For He says to Moses, "I WILL HAVE MERCY ON WHOMEVER I WILL HAVE MERCY, AND I WILL HAVE COMPASSION ON WHOMEVER I WILL HAVE COMPASSION." So then it is not of him who wills, nor of him who runs, but of God who shows mercy.

For the Scripture says to the Pharaoh, "FOR THIS VERY PURPOSE I HAVE RAISED YOU UP, THAT I MAY SHOW MY POWER IN YOU, AND THAT MY NAME MAY BE DECLARED IN ALL THE EARTH."

Therefore He has mercy on whom He wills, and whom He wills He hardens. You will say to me then, "Why does He still find fault? For who has resisted His will?"

But indeed, O man, who are you to reply against God? Will the thing formed say to him who formed it, "Why have you made me like this?" Does not the potter have power over the clay, from the same lump to make one vessel for honor and another for dishonor?

What if God, wanting to show His wrath and to make His power known, endured with much longsuffering the vessels of wrath prepared for destruction, and that He might make known the riches of His glory on the vessels of mercy, which He had prepared beforehand for glory, even us whom He called, not of the Jews only, but also of the Gentiles?"

(Romans 9: 13-24)

57

Now, if we are sincere, even with the knowledge that it is useless to struggle with God, many withdraw in silence and the bitter feeling of dissatisfaction with the Apostle's explanation...

...disquieted as they sense that God has not answered their questions.

Notwithstanding, **God has made it clear** that He desires that all obtain and understand the knowledge of His ways.

He has said::

> *"Thus says the LORD: "Let not the wise man glory in his wisdom, Let not the mighty man glory in his might, Nor let the rich man glory in his riches; But let him who glories glory in this, That he* **understands and knows Me**, *That I am the LORD, <u>exercising lovingkindness, judgment, and righteousness in the earth</u>. For in these I delight," says the LORD"* (Jeremiah 9: 23-24)

The risk is enormous when we know nothing of God, for we choose to expose ourselves to severe judgment, following those who live in a riotous manner and away from the purposes of God.

> *"Hear the word of the LORD, You children of Israel, For the LORD brings a charge against the inhabitants of the land: "<u>There is no truth or mercy Or knowledge of God in the land</u>.*
>
> *By swearing and lying, Killing and stealing and committing adultery, They break all restraint, With bloodshed upon bloodshed.*
>
> *Therefore the land will mourn; And everyone who dwells there will waste away...*
>
> *... **My people are destroyed for lack of knowledge ...**"* (Hosea 4: 1-6)

The fact that God, in His sovereign will, created man in His image and likeness (Gen. 1:26); and breathed through his nostrils the "**breathe of life**" to make him a "**living soul**" (*Hebrew=Nefesh*) (Gen. 2:7); and made us "*a little less than the angels*" (Hebrews 2:7), has many ramifications for humanity.

He made us each unique beings and gave us free will; subjecting His own grace and righteousness to the choice made by each human being. He is aware of the weakness of our flesh, but enables us to overcome.

He watches as the "Tempter" seeks the destruction and devastation of every living soul:

> "*Be sober, be vigilant; because your adversary the devil walks about like a roaring lion, seeking whom he may devour.*"
> *(1 Peter 5:8),*

And he has demonstrated His faithfulness:

> "*No temptation has overtaken you except such as is common to man; but God is faithful, who will not allow you to be tempted beyond what you are able, but with the temptation will also make the way of escape, that you may be able to bear it.*"
> (1 Corinthians 10:13)

> "*And He said to me, "My grace is sufficient for you, for My strength is made perfect in weakness." Therefore most gladly I will rather boast in my infirmities, that the power of Christ may rest upon me*" (2 Corinthians 12:9)

In answer to the questions posed previously; **I do believe** that God knows all things but <u>in His sovereign wisdom</u> **chose to refrain from using this knowledge and rather abstained from knowing what choices each person would make**; thus giving each the privilege of free will *(those in heaven as well as those on earth)*. He holds everyone responsible for their choices and will one day judge each person accordingly, based on their actions.

For this reason we read expressions of amazement and earnest expectation from God as he observes an unexpected decision against His will from an individual, and as He awaits the response of a person or nation after, in His mercy, he has sent them a particular message.

It is thus so, when we read in the Bible:

" *God is not a man, that He should lie, Nor a son of man, that He should repent. Has He said, and will He not do? Or has He spoken, and will He not make it good?* " (Numbers 23:19)

If anyone should pause and question: Why do we read in other biblical passages that He repented of something?

"Then the LORD saw that the wickedness of man was great in the earth, and that every intent of the thoughts of his heart was only evil continually. And the LORD was sorry that He had made man on the earth, and He was grieved in His heart."
(Genesis 6: 5-6)

"Then God saw their works, that they turned from their evil way; and God relented from the disaster that He had said He would bring upon them, and He did not do it…" (Jonah 3:10)

… So he prayed to the LORD, and said, "Ah, LORD, was not this what I said when I was still in my country? Therefore I fled previously to Tarshish; for I know that You are a gracious and merciful God, slow to anger and abundant in lovingkindness, One who relents from doing harm. (Jonah 4:2)

The Word of God gives us an explanation when and why He turns from doing something (repents)

The Word of God gives us an explanation when and why He turns from doing something (repents)

*"The instant I speak concerning a nation and concerning a kingdom, to pluck up, to pull down, and to destroy it, <u>if that nation against whom I have spoken turns from its evil</u>, **I will relent of** the disaster that I thought to bring upon it.*
And the instant I speak concerning a nation and concerning a kingdom, to build and to plant it, if it does evil in My sight so that it does not obey My voice, then I will relent concerning the good with which I said I would benefit it."   (Jeremiah 18: 7-10)

"In the beginning of the reign of Jehoiakim the son of Josiah, king of Judah, this word came from the LORD, saying, "Thus says the LORD: 'Stand in the court of the LORD's house, and speak to all the cities of Judah, which come to worship in the LORD's house, all the words that I command you to speak to them. Do not diminish a word.

<u>*Perhaps everyone will listen and turn from his evil way*</u>*, **that I may relent concerning the calamity which I purpose to bring on them** because of the evil of their doings.'*   (Jeremiah 26: 1-3)

... Now therefore, amend your ways and your doings, and obey the voice of the LORD your God, then the LORD will relent concerning the doom that He has pronounced against you."
(Jeremiah 26:13)

We will examine the life of King Ahab *(one of the most apostate of the kings of Israel)*. After the prophet Elijah was sent by God to tell him the type of punishment prepared for him, Ahab humbled himself and this was the response:

"So Ahab said to Elijah, "Have you found me, O my enemy?" And he answered, "I have found you, because you have sold yourself to do evil in the sight of the LORD:
'Behold, I will bring calamity on you. I will take away your posterity, and will cut off from Ahab every male in Israel, both bond and free.

63

I will make your house like the house of Jeroboam the son of Nebat, and like the house of Baasha the son of Ahijah, because of the provocation with which you have provoked Me to anger, and made Israel sin.'

And concerning Jezebel the LORD also spoke, saying, 'The dogs shall eat Jezebel by the wall of Jezreel.'
The dogs shall eat whoever belongs to Ahab and dies in the city, and the birds of the air shall eat whoever dies in the field."

But there was no one like Ahab who sold himself to do wickedness in the sight of the LORD, because Jezebel his wife stirred him up. And he behaved very abominably in following idols, according to all that the Amorites had done, whom the LORD had cast out before the children of Israel.

So it was, when Ahab heard those words, that he tore his clothes and put sackcloth on his body, and fasted and lay in sackcloth, and went about mourning.

And the word of the LORD came to Elijah the Tishbite, saying, "See how Ahab has humbled himself before Me? <u>Because he has humbled himself before Me,</u> I will not bring the calamity in his days. In the days of his son I will bring the calamity on his house." (1 Kings 21: 20-29)

Throughout all the verses we notice a common denominator:

<< God works justice and righteousness upon the earth; but above all, He delights in showing mercy.

Before any punishment, He will reveal the areas that require correction; and if the person that committed any evil should repent of his actions with all his heart and makes a decision to abandon that erroneous course of action; the way of God is to repent of the punishment He had before declared. >>

The key element here is: Make a decision to abandon that sinful behavior and in genuine repentance; receive forgiveness from God. If there is no turning away from sin, God then must execute judgment against us, as He has spoken it.

> *"'The LORD is longsuffering and abundant in mercy, forgiving iniquity and transgression; but He <u>by no means clears the guilty</u>...*" (Numbers 14:18ₐ)

> *"The LORD is slow to anger and great in power, And <u>will not at all acquit the wicked.</u>"* (Nahum 1:3)

THERE IS SOMETHING ELSE TO CONSIDER:

A just human being has never existed?

The majority of those who defend the dogma of original sin give it an absolutist interpretation, which is responded to by Apostle Paul in Romans 3:

> *"As it is written: "THERE IS NONE RIGHTEOUS, NO, NOT ONE; THERE IS NONE WHO UNDERSTANDS; THERE IS NONE WHO SEEKS AFTER GOD. THEY HAVE ALL TURNED ASIDE; THEY HAVE TOGETHER BECOME UNPROFITABLE; THERE IS NONE WHO DOES GOOD, NO, NOT ONE."* (Romans 3: 10-12)

They believe and teach this interpretation of Paul's writings: "as in fact all are born being sinners, apart from the Lord Jesus, there is presently no one, nor at any other time in human history someone of which it could be said was justified by his own righteousness."

Nevertheless, this is not what the Bible has to say.

It does say that during the time Paul wrote these words, no one sought God...; neither Jew nor gentile. The condition of the people was the same as when David wrote of all having strayed from the fold:

"The fool has said in his heart, "There is no God." They are corrupt, They have done abominable works, There is none who does good. The LORD looks down from heaven upon the children of men, To see if there are any who understand, who seek God. They have all turned aside, They have together become corrupt; There is none who does good, No, not one." (Psalm 14: 1-3)

The Bible also tells us that God declared some as righteous, because of their own righteousness:

"The word of the LORD came again to me, saying:
"Son of man, when a land sins against Me by persistent unfaithfulness, I will stretch out My hand against it; I will cut off its supply of bread, send famine on it, and cut off man and beast from it.
Even if these three men, Noah, Daniel, and Job, were in it, they would deliver only themselves by their righteousness," says the Lord GOD. ...

"Or if I send a pestilence into that land and pour out My fury on it in blood, and cut off from it man and beast, even though Noah, Daniel, and Job were in it, as I live," says the Lord GOD, "they would deliver neither son nor daughter; they would deliver only themselves by their righteousness." (Ezequiel 14: 12-14, 19-20)

As we turn to the historical biblical narrative we find that Noah, Daniel, and Job lived pleasing lives before God; but in all this, their righteousness was very limited and they were unable to as much as save their own sons/daughters.

There is an enormous difference in the perfect righteousness imputed through our Lord Jesus, whereas all humanity can find justification in His righteousness.

"But the free gift is not like the offense. For if by the one man's offense many died, much more the grace of God and the gift by the grace of the one Man, Jesus Christ, abounded to many.

And the gift is not like that which came through the one who sinned. For the judgment which came from one offense resulted in condemnation, but the free gift which came from many offenses resulted in justification.

*For if by the one man's offense death reigned through the one, much more **those who receive** abundance of grace and of the gift of righteousness will reign in life through the One, Jesus Christ.)*

Therefore, as through one man's offense judgment came to all men, resulting in condemnation, <u>even so through one Man's righteous act the free gift came to all men, resulting in justification of life.</u>

For as by one man's disobedience many were made sinners, so also by one Man's obedience many will be made righteous.

Moreover the law entered that the offense might abound. But where sin abounded, grace abounded much more, so that as sin reigned in death, even so grace might reign through righteousness to eternal life through Jesus Christ our Lord."

(Romans 5: 15-21)

"THANKS BE TO GOD FOR HIS UNSPEAKABLE GIFT!"

(2 Corinthians 9:15)

Let us continue and enter into the waters of biblical revelation. We will proceed and analyze the grace of God and our salvation from a totally biblical perspective, but not with the same focus we have grown accustomed to hearing!

Salvation:

The story that is continually written

Salvation: The story that is continually written

If there is an important theme we may trace through the Bible from the fall of man by disobedience, it is the story of salvation.

We see that before banishing Adam and Eve from paradise, God gave them the promise of redemption when He told the serpent *(Satan, also Rev.12:29 and Ezekiel 28:13)* that the seed of woman would bruise his head.

It was also prophesized that a child would be born of a virgin:

"Therefore the Lord himself shall give you a sign; Behold, a virgin shall conceive, and bear a son, and shall call his name Immanuel." (This means "God with us")   (Isaiah 7:14)

Isaiah also tells us that the child shall be a prince and shall be acknowledged in an extraordinary manner:

"For unto us a child is born, unto us a son is given: and the government shall be upon his shoulder: and his name shall be called Wonderful, Counselor, The mighty God, The everlasting Father, The Prince of peace."   (Isaiah 9:6)

The Bible declares that Jesus was born of a virgin woman; **Mary**, the blessed of God and among all woman by the declaration of faith made to the angel Gabriel (Luke 1:28)

Jesus was born, grew, and fulfilled all the purpose of His coming to this world: To **Redeem** all humanity and **Restore** all things.

Apostle Peter wrote on one occasion:

> *"This is the stone which was set at naught of you builders, which is become the head of the corner. Neither is there salvation in any other: for **there is none other name** under heaven given among men, whereby we must be saved"*
> (Acts 4:11-12)

On another occasion, the Apostle Paul declares:

> *"… that is, the word of faith, which we preach; That if thou shalt confess with thy mouth the Lord Jesus, and shalt believe in thine heart that God hath raised him from the dead, thou shalt be saved… **For whosoever shall call upon the name of the Lord shall be saved.**"* (Romans 10: 8^b-13)

The same Jesus said:

> *"For God so loved the world, that he gave his only begotten Son, **that whosoever believeth in him** should not perish, but have everlasting life. For God sent not his Son into the world to condemn the world; but that the world through him might be saved."* *(John 3:16-17)*

> *"For I came down from heaven, not to do mine own will, but the will of him that sent me. And **this is the Father's will** which hath sent me, that of all which he hath given me I should lose nothing, but should raise it up again at the last day.*

> *"And this is the will of him that sent me, that every one which seeth the Son, and believeth on him, may have everlasting life: and I will raise him up at the last day."* *(John 6:38-40)*

> *"And if any man hear my words, and believe not, I judge him not: for I came not to judge the world, **but to save** the world."*
> *(John 12:47)*

We should take note there is a great revelation in these words.

They all speak of the salvation offered to **all** human beings who would believe on the name of Jesus and would acknowledge Him as Lord. A person's race or social standing is irrelevant, although it was not always this way.

There was a time when the promises of God were for one people exclusively: The Jews. To better understand why God did this, let us read the biblical narrative.

Generational blessings and their transfer

A brief historical analysis of the Biblical Timeline:

In the creation, God placed Adam in Eden or Paradise; then created a woman as a companion and married them *(Gen.2:7, 8, 15, 18, 21-25)*

He then **blessed them** *(Gen.1:28)* by pure grace and love, as God had created them so they may have communion with Him.

When the man disobeyed God's commandment, man was cursed, along with the earth and the serpent *(Gen.3:3-17)*

Men then became so corrupt that God repented of having created man on the earth *(Gen.6:6)* and decided to destroy all on the earth: man, beast, and reptiles, fowl… All!

Nevertheless, we read that although he was surrounded by such a sinful society, there was a man who found grace before the eyes of God *(Gen 6:8)* as he loved God, sought Him and desired to please Him. **His name was Noah.**

God made a pact with Noah (Gen. 6:18); **and passed him the blessing** *(Gen. 9:1)* that he had before given to Adam and Eve.

However, in the second blessing that God gave to the humanity through Noah, He did not give back *the dominion* usurped by Satan to Adam.

Compare Genesis 1:28 to Genesis 9:1:

> *"Then God blessed them, and God said to them, "Be fruitful and multiply; fill the earth and subdue it; **have dominion** over the fish of the sea, over the birds of the air, and over every living thing that moves on the earth.""* (Genesis 1:28)

> *"So God blessed Noah and his sons, and said to them: "Be fruitful and multiply, and fill the earth."* (Genesis 9:1)

This is why in the desert, when addressing Christ concerning this dominion *(Luke 4:5-6)*, the Lord did not accuse him as stating a lie but acknowledged, shamefully, that such dominion Satan had was valid.

> *"Then the devil, taking Him up on a high mountain, showed Him all the kingdoms of the world in a moment of time.*
> *And the devil said to Him, "All this authority I will give You, and their glory; <u>for this has been delivered to me</u>,... "* (Luke 4: 5-6)

In spite of this, the Bible declares that afterwards, **when Jesus Christ died on the cross...**

...All the authority Satan had was taken by Christ:

> *"...having wiped out the handwriting of requirements that was against us, which was contrary to us. And He has taken it out of the way, having nailed it to the cross. Having disarmed principalities and powers, He made a public spectacle of them, triumphing over them in it."* (Coloss. 2: 14-15)

> *"But one of the elders said to me, "Do not weep. Behold, the Lion of the tribe of Judah, the Root of David, has prevailed to open the scroll and to loose its seven seals."* (Revelation 5:5)

... And is **now shared with the Church**:

"...that you may know what is the hope of His calling, what are the riches of the glory of His inheritance in the saints, and what is the exceeding greatness of His power toward us who believe, according to the working of His mighty power which He worked in Christ when He raised Him from the dead and seated Him at His right hand in the heavenly places, far above all principality and power and might and dominion, and every name that is named, not only in this age but also in that which is to come.

And He put all things under His feet, and gave Him to be head over all things to the church, which is His body, the fullness of Him who fills all in all." (Ephesians 1: 18-23)

"But God, who is rich in mercy, because of His great love with which He loved us, even when we were dead in trespasses, made us alive together with Christ (by grace you have been saved), and raised us up together, and made us sit together in the heavenly places in Christ Jesus, that in the ages to come He might show the exceeding riches of His grace in His kindness toward us in Christ Jesus." (Ephesians 2: 4-7)

"...to the intent that now the manifold wisdom of God might be made known by the church to the principalities and powers in the heavenly places, according to the eternal purpose which He accomplished in Christ Jesus our Lord, in whom we have boldness and access with confidence through faith in Him."
(Ephesians 3: 10-12)

Firmness rewards you

GOD IS RIGHTEOUS; and **it is worth** choosing to live without allowing oneself to be dragged through the mud by the currents of this world.

That person who will live righteously will be rewarded. God will honor his faith and obedience. Noah is a living and real example.

The Bible states in the book of 2 Chronicles that:

> *"For the eyes of the Lord run to and fro throughout the whole earth, to show himself strong in the behalf of them whose heart is perfect toward him. "* (2 Chron.16:9)

Due to the manner in which Noah chose to live, humanity and all species of animals and fowl were not extinguished.

Let us take note of the blessing Noah obtained **by obeying** all that God had told him *(Gen.6:22),* and then passed to his son **Shem** *(Gen. 9:26).*

The blessing was passed from one generation to the next generation *(Gen.11:10-31)* and much later the moment arrived when God decided to separate unto Him a holy people, set apart from unrighteousness.

The Bible relates that **Abram**, son of Terah, **descendant of Shem**, was called by God and instructed to leave the land of his fathers and go to a place He would show him; and God would bless him.

We see that now the blessing of God would take on further significance:

God decided to raise a people that would have his blessing and chose Abram (whose name He later changed to Abraham, which means *"father of a multitude" (Gen. 17:1-5)* and he would be the patriarch of this blessed people *(whom we now recognize as Jews).*

A very interesting situation:

We have an interesting point here: God had spoken directly to Abraham and promised him great blessings *(Gen.12:1-4),* if Abraham obeyed... and Abraham responded by obeying.

(The Bible states that through Abraham's obedience, his faith was counted for righteousness *(Romans 4:3; Heb 11:8)*;

Nevertheless, God had to test the faith of Abraham in a peculiar manner; **and it was not until Abraham obeyed** and passed the test, that God swore to him with an oath that he would receive the blessing as promised. *(Gen.22: 1-18; Heb.11:17-19)*

IN OUR DAYS, WE HAVE BEEN BLESSED FURTHER as a result of Jesus Christ's perfect obedience in life, who:

> *"...who, though he was in the form of God, did not count equality with God a thing to be grasped, but emptied himself, by taking the form of a servant, being born in the likeness of men.*
>
> *And being found in human form, he humbled himself by **becoming obedient to the point of death**, even death on a cross."*
> (Philippians 2: 5-8, ASV)

> *"...He disarmed the rulers and authorities and put them to open shame, **by triumphing over them** in him."* (Coloss. 2:15, ASV).

God has extended his blessing that it may cover all humanity (without regard to race or nation), so that they may receive His grace and forgiveness for sin on the merits of the Lord Jesus Christ.

> *"The true light, which gives light to everyone, was coming into the world... **But to all who did receive him, who believed in his name, he gave the right to become children of God***"
> (John 1: 9-12, ASV)

> *"Therefore **it is of faith** that it might be according to grace so that the promise might be sure to all the seed, not only to those who are of the law, but also to those who are of the faith of Abraham, who is the father of us all...*
>
> *And therefore "IT WAS ACCOUNTED TO HIM FOR RIGHTEOUSNESS."*

Now it was not written for his sake alone *that it was imputed to him,* ***but also for us.***

It shall be imputed to us who believe in Him who raised up Jesus our Lord from the dead, who was delivered up because of our offenses, and was raised because of our justification.

(Romans 4: 16, 22,25)

"<u>But now in Christ Jesus</u> you who once were far off have been brought near by the blood of Christ....

"And He came and preached peace to you who were afar off and to those who were near. <u>For through Him we both have access by one Spirit to the Father</u>... " (Ephesians 2: 11-22)

"Therefore, as through one man's offense judgment came to all men, resulting in condemnation, even so <u>through one Man's righteous act</u> the free gift came to all men, ***resulting in justification of life.*** *"* (Romanos 5:18).

Does this mean that the entire world is now automatically justified before God?

The answer is: **NO!**

But **everyone in the world has the opportunity** of being justified, as the Apostle Peter said:

"The Lord is not slack concerning His promise, as some count slackness, but is longsuffering toward us, not willing that any should perish but that all should come to repentance."

(2 Peter 3:9)

What would then be the Meaning of Salvation?

What would then be the meaning of salvation?

Apostle Paul writes that a soul can find themselves in one of two situations: the Natural man, or the Spiritual Man.

> *"But the <u>natural</u> man does not receive the things of the Spirit of God, for they are foolishness to him; nor can he know them, because they are spiritually discerned.*
>
> *But he who is <u>spiritual</u> judges all things, yet he himself is rightly judged by no one. For "WHO HAS KNOWN THE MIND OF THE LORD THAT HE MAY INSTRUCT HIM?" But we have the mind of Christ"* (1 Corinthians 2: 14-16)

Further on he writes that spiritual growth necessitates a willingness to go through a process; which is initiated and perfected by the Holy Spirit.

> *"...being confident of this very thing, that He who has begun a good work in you will complete it until the day of Jesus Christ..."* (Philippians 1:6)

After a person is born again of the Spirit *(John 3:3-8)*, he or she is considered a spiritual "babe" (infant); and for a time their spiritual perception be in error, they make mistakes, and may even falter or fall at times. They are learning how to "live and walk in the Spirit."

(See: Romans 8:1-17; Galatians 3:25-29; 4:1-7; Titus 3: 3-5)

There is an expectation that the time will come where spiritual maturity has been developed and the person is no longer subject to carnal desires that directed their life before obtaining the grace of God.

> *"...of whom we have much to say, and hard to explain, since you have become dull of hearing. For though by this time you ought to be teachers, you need someone to teach you again the first principles of the oracles of God; and you have come to need milk*

and not solid food. For everyone who partakes only of milk is unskilled in the word of righteousness, for he is a babe.

But solid food belongs to those who are of full age, that is, those who by reason of use have their senses exercised to discern both good and evil." (Hebrews 5: 11-14)

*"Therefore, since Christ suffered for us in the flesh, arm yourselves also with the same mind, for he who has suffered in the flesh has ceased from sin, **that he no longer should live the rest of his time in the flesh for the lusts of men, but for the will of God.***

***For we have spent enough of our past lifetime in doing the will of the Gentiles**—when we walked in lewdness, lusts, drunkenness, revelries, drinking parties, and abominable idolatries.*
In regard to these, they think it strange that you do not run with them in the same flood of dissipation, speaking evil of you.
They will give an account to Him who is ready to judge the living and the dead." (1 Peter 4: 1-5)

This is the reason Apostle Paul scolded the church at Corinth when their actions demonstrated they were still "babes in Christ", instead of living as spiritual men and women.

*"And I, brethren, could not speak to you as to spiritual people but as to carnal, as to babes in Christ. I fed you with milk and not with solid food; for until now you were not able to receive it, and even now you are still not able; for **you are still carnal**. For where there are envy, strife, and divisions among you, are you not carnal and behaving like mere men?* (1 Corinthians 3: 1-3)

In other words, the behavior of the Corinthians showed them as still being carnal and not spiritual. Paul specifically spoke of some of their works and identified them as jealous, contentious, and having dissentions among them.

Many believers do not realize that the practice of what has been described as the works of the flesh will stunt their spiritual growth, and as well as paralyzing them spiritually they are in the egregious risk of forfeiting the precious grace given them by the merits of the Lord Jesus Christ.

There is an urgency to live in subjection to the Spirit.

All carnal behavior must be brought in subjection to the Spirit, so it no longer lives in us.

"Therefore, brethren, we are debtors—not to the flesh, to live according to the flesh. For if you live according to the flesh you will die; but if by the Spirit you put to death the deeds of the body, you will live." (Romans 8: 12-13)

"For all the law is fulfilled in one word, even in this: "YOU SHALL LOVE YOUR NEIGHBOR AS YOURSELF." But if you bite and devour one another, beware lest you be consumed by one another!
I say then: Walk in the Spirit, and you shall not fulfill the lust of the flesh. For the flesh lusts against the Spirit, and the Spirit against the flesh; and these are contrary to one another, so that you do not do the things that you wish.

But if you are led by the Spirit, you are not under the law.
*Now the works of the flesh are evident, which are: adultery, fornication, uncleanness, lewdness, idolatry, sorcery, hatred, contentions, jealousies, outbursts of wrath, selfish ambitions, dissensions, heresies, envy, murders, drunkenness, revelries, and the like; of which I tell you beforehand, just as I also told you in time past, that **those who practice such things will not inherit the kingdom of God.**"* (Galatians 5: 14-21)

To live in Disobedience to the Holy Spirit is to be Rebellious; And the Consequences are Devastating:

"For if we sin willfully after we have received the knowledge of the truth, there no longer remains a sacrifice for sins, but a certain fearful expectation of judgment, and fiery indignation which will devour the adversaries.

Anyone who has rejected Moses' law dies without mercy on the testimony of two or three witnesses.

*Of how much worse punishment, do you suppose, will he be
thought worthy who has trampled the Son of God underfoot,
counted the blood of the covenant by which he was sanctified a
common thing, and insulted the Spirit of grace?*

*For we know Him who said, "VENGEANCE IS MINE, I WILL REPAY,"
says the Lord. And again, "THE LORD WILL JUDGE HIS PEOPLE."
It is a fearful thing to fall into the hands of the living God."*
(Hebrews 10: 26-31)

Serious study of the Holy Bible is the path that must be taken
by a believer who desires to grow and mature in faith. Here it is
where we learn to consciously apply the Scriptures to every area
of our life, as the Holy Spirit guides us.

*"But you must continue in the things which you have learned and
been assured of, knowing from whom you have learned them,
and that from childhood you have known the Holy Scriptures,
which are able to make you wise for salvation through faith
which is in Christ Jesus.*

*All Scripture is given by inspiration of God, and is profitable for
doctrine, for reproof, for correction, for instruction in
righteousness, that the man of God may be complete, thoroughly
equipped for every good work."* (2 Timothy 3: 14-17)

Lord Jesus said:

"...But he who endures to the end shall be saved."
(Matthew 24: 11-13)

Peter also said:

*"...In this you greatly rejoice, though now for a little while, if
need be, you have been grieved by various trials, that the
genuineness of your faith, being much more precious than gold
that perishes, though it is tested by fire, may be found to praise,
honor, and glory at the revelation of Jesus Christ, whom having
not seen you love. Though now you do not see Him, yet believing,
you rejoice with joy inexpressible and full of glory, **receiving the
end of your faith—the salvation of your souls."*** (1 Peter 1: 6-9)

84

And in the book of Hebrews we have this advice:

"Beware, brethren, lest there be in any of you an evil heart of unbelief in departing from the living God... For we have become partakers of Christ if we hold the beginning of our confidence steadfast to the end" (Hebrews 3: 12-14)

The Bible speaks to us in exhortation as to how our manner of life should be. Now, after having read these verses we go on to answer the question, what does it mean to be saved?

The best way I can use to **explain salvation** is to compare it to an IMMIGRANT VISA that allows a particular person to enter and live in a country, and then apply for citizenship

There are **requirements** that must be satisfied for them to obtain the VISA (and in acquiring it, the person then has a **privilege**); and in addition, there are norms that must be respected and obeyed in order to not lose this privilege.

The Bible demonstrates we all have access to the Father by one Spirit and we are part of His family, people, and kingdom *(Ephesians 2:18);* nevertheless, before coming to Christ we were sinful and malicious.

"that at that time you were without Christ, being aliens from the commonwealth of Israel and strangers from the covenants of promise, having no hope and without God in the world."
(Ephesians 2:12).

The Word has more to say of our **manner of life before**:

"For we ourselves were also once foolish, disobedient, deceived, serving various lusts and pleasures, living in malice and envy, hateful and hating one another " (Titus 3:3)

"...being filled with all unrighteousness, sexual immorality, wickedness, covetousness, maliciousness; full of envy, murder, strife, deceit, evil-mindedness; they are whisperers, backbiters, haters of God, violent, proud, boasters, inventors of evil things, disobedient to parents, undiscerning, untrustworthy, unloving, unforgiving, unmerciful" (Romans 1: 29-31)

" ...deceiving and being deceived.." (2 Timothy 3:13)

The following chart demonstrates the weight of sin on our soul, If we lack the grace of God:

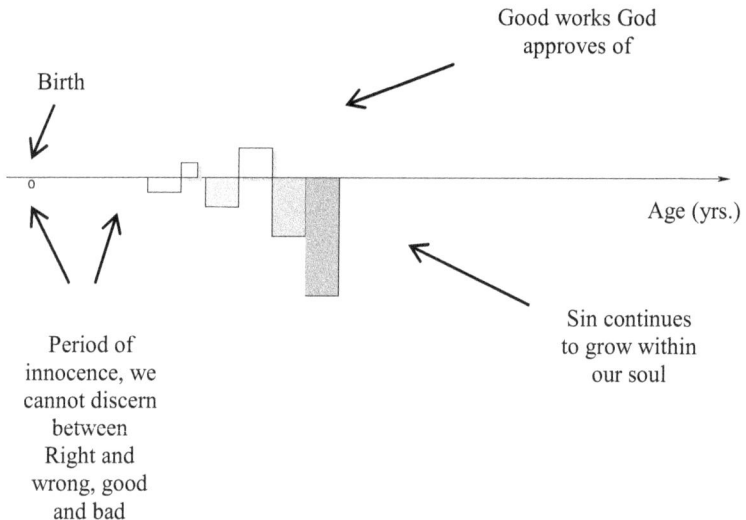

Good works God
approves of

Birth

0

Age (yrs.)

Sin continues
to grow within
our soul

Period of
innocence, we
cannot discern
between
Right and
wrong, good
and bad

86

Let us bear in mind that God knows our hearts

*"**The heart** is deceitful above all things, and desperately wicked: who can know it? I the LORD search the heart, I try the reins, even to give every man **according to his ways**, and according to the fruit of his doings.* " (Jeremiah 17:9-10)

"'The LORD is longsuffering and abundant in mercy, forgiving iniquity and transgression; but He by no means clears the guilty...'" (Numbers 14:18)

God had said beforehand, **He desires not the death of sinner**, but that he would repent:

*"... Say unto them, As I live, saith the Lord GOD, <u>I have no pleasure in the death of the wicked</u>; **but that the wicked turn from his way and live:** turn ye, turn ye from your evil ways; for why will ye die, O house of Israel?* " (Ezekiel 33:10-11)

*"The Lord is not slack concerning his promise, as some men count slackness; but is **longsuffering** to us-ward, <u>not willing that any should perish</u>, but that all should come to repentance. "*
(2 Peter 3:9)

We conclude, when someone is repentant of all their transgressions, and asks for forgiveness of God putting their faith in Jesus Christ, the Bible says:

""Wash yourselves, make yourselves clean; Put away the evil of your doings from before My eyes. Cease to do evil, Learn to do good; Seek justice, Rebuke the oppressor; Defend the fatherless, Plead for the widow.

"Come now, and let us reason together," Says the LORD, "Though your sins are like scarlet, They shall be as white as snow; Though they are red like crimson, They shall be as wool. "
(Isaiah 1: 16-18)

"...the blood of Jesus Christ His Son cleanses us from all sin ... If we confess our sins, He is faithful and just to forgive us our sins and to cleanse us from all unrighteousness." (1 John 1: 7, 9)

Graph of how the burden of sin is lifted from our soul, after we receive forgiveness of God by faith in Christ.

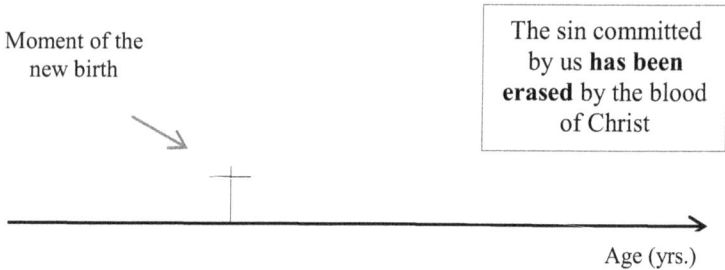

Moment of the
new birth

The sin committed
by us **has been**
erased by the blood
of Christ

Age (yrs.)

This means when we come to God after recognizing all the wrongs we've committed, and in an attitude of repentance ask forgiveness for our sins, the Bible says **we are born again of God in the Spirit** and all things are made new in us:

"... Jesus answered and said to him, "Most assuredly, I say to you, unless one is born again, he cannot see the kingdom of God." Nicodemus said to Him, "How can a man be born when he is old?

Can he enter a second time into his mother's womb and be born?" Jesus answered, "Most assuredly, I say to you, unless one is born of water and the Spirit, he cannot enter the kingdom of God.

That which is born of the flesh is flesh, and that which is born of the Spirit is spirit. Do not marvel that I said to you, 'You must be born again.' ... " (John 3: 3-8)

"Therefore, if anyone is in Christ, he is a new creation; old things have passed away; behold, all things have become new.
(2 Corinthians 5:17)

In other words, God enables us to
START OVER AGAIN

The difference is now we are given an **enormous advantage**.

Now the **Holy Spirit** lives within us and He will **teach** us to live correctly, as God wills.

After we initially confess and receive forgiveness of sin, the Holy Spirit will **convict** of habitual sin and instill a desire to quickly repent of any sinful actions. Any prior stronghold of sin will be overcome and have **no dominion** over us.

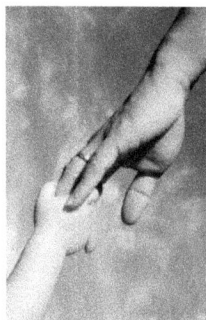

The Bible says:

"Therefore **do not let sin reign** *in your mortal body, that you should obey it in its lusts. And do not present your members as instruments of unrighteousness to sin, but present yourselves to God as being alive from the dead, and your members as instruments of righteousness to God. For* **sin shall not have dominion over you**, *for you are not under law but under grace.*
(Romans 6: 12-14)

"...when He, the Spirit of truth, has come, He will guide you into all truth..." (John 16:13)

And, What About The Future Sins?

A common error in interpreting Scripture is a belief that all our **FUTURE** sins are instantly forgiven when we receive Christ as our personal Savior.

Those with this belief put forth that when Christ died for us on the cross of Calvary; all our sins were still in the future and were paid for.

This is an immature understanding of God and his pact with humanity, as He declares in His Word that He is not mocked:

> *"Do not be deceived, God is not mocked; for whatever a man sows, that he will also reap. For **he who sows to his flesh will of the flesh reap corruption,** but he who sows to the Spirit will of the Spirit reap everlasting life"* (Galatians 6: 7-8)

What the Bible does say is:

> *"But now the righteousness of God apart from the law is revealed, being witnessed by the Law and the Prophets, even the righteousness of God, **through faith in Jesus Christ,** to all and on all who believe*
>
> *"For there is no difference; for all have sinned and fall short of the glory of God, being justified freely by His grace through the redemption that is in Christ Jesus...*
>
> *... whom God set forth as a propitiation **by His blood,** through faith, to demonstrate His righteousness, because in His forbearance God had passed over **the sins that were previously committed,** to demonstrate at the present time His righteousness, that He might be just and the justifier of the one who has faith in Jesus."* (Romans 3: 21-26)

> *"For he who lacks these things is shortsighted, even to blindness, and has forgotten that he was cleansed from **his old sins"*** (2 Peter 1:9)

What then occurs when a Christian sins after receiving the grace of God in his life?

We should continually examine ourselves in our daily walk (*examine yourself with care*, Paul told young Timothy, *1Tim. 4:16); and* avoid all rebellion in our behavior towards the Holy Spirit by all means.

> *"Therefore gird up the loins of your mind, be sober, and rest your hope fully upon the grace that is to be brought to you at the revelation of Jesus Christ; as obedient children, **not conforming yourselves to the former lusts**, as in your ignorance; but as He who called you is holy, you also be holy in all your conduct, because it is written, "BE HOLY, FOR I AM HOLY."*
> *And if you call on the Father, who **without partiality judges according to each one's work**, conduct yourselves throughout the time of your stay here in fear"* (1 Peter 1: 13-17)

Even so, the Bible clearly shows that Christian believers will sin in this life *(though involuntarily);* and forgiveness from sin through Christ is their only solution:

> *"If we say that we have no sin, we deceive ourselves, and the truth is not in us."* (1 John 1:8)

To further explain, if we do commit an act of sin *(and there is none who will not, as we are not perfect but are perfected),* our soul has the **blemish** of this sin; but on recognizing and repenting of it, we ask forgiveness of God, and He forgives and washes us, maintaining us pure before Him.

> *"...If we confess our sins, He is faithful and just to forgive us our sins and to cleanse us from all unrighteousness."*
> *"the blood of Jesus Christ His Son cleanses us from all sin..."*
> (1 John 1: 9, 7)

> *"When I shut up heaven and there is no rain, or command the locusts to devour the land, or send pestilence among My people, if My people who are called by My name will humble themselves, and pray and seek My face, and turn from their wicked ways, then I will hear from heaven, and will forgive their sin and heal their land"* (2 Chr. 7: 13-14)

The Unnatural Procedure

The Unnatural Procedure

Subsequently, we will say that it is **unnatural** for a true Christian to continue a life of sin. There is no habitual sin. This is what the Word has to say:

> *"He who sins is of the devil, for the devil has sinned from the beginning. For this purpose the Son of God was manifested, that He might destroy the works of the devil.*
>
> *Whoever has been born of God does not sin, for His seed remains in him; and he cannot sin, because he has been born of God."* (1 Juan 3: 8-9)

> *"You are of God, little children, and have overcome them, because **He who is in you is greater** than he who is in the world.*
> (1 John 4:4)

> *"Yet in all these things **we are more than conquerors** through Him who loved us.."* (Romans 8:37)

Whosoever is born of God does not practice sin; to reiterate, does not sin habitually. There is not a continual practice of sin as the sons of perdition do.

The true Christian puts off sin and grows spiritually, knowing that all practice of sin affects their faith negatively and imperils their soul.

Now, based on what the Word says:

> *"Pursue peace with all people, and holiness, without which no one will see the Lord:"* (Hebrews 12:14)

> *"Beloved, I beg you as sojourners and pilgrims, abstain from fleshly lusts which <u>war against the soul</u>, having your conduct honorable among the Gentiles, that when they speak against you as evildoers, they may, by your good works which they observe, glorify God in the day of visitation."* (1 Peter 2: 11-12)

95

We should remember the Bible says that sin brings forth death; not only sins we consider "**BIG**":

> "...but if you show partiality, you commit sin, and are **convicted** by the law as transgressors.
>
> For whoever shall keep the whole law, and yet stumble in one point, he is **guilty of all**. For He who said, "DO NOT COMMIT ADULTERY," also said, "DO NOT MURDER." Now if you do not commit adultery, but you do murder, you have become a transgressor of the law. So speak and so do as those who will be judged by the law of liberty. For judgment is without mercy to the one who has shown no mercy. **Mercy triumphs over judgment.**"
>
> (James 2: 8-13)

We see that God will **chastise** believers and there is judgment for disobedience, allowing them to **escape** the greater condemnation of the final "judgment day."

The Bible says:

"*the wages of sin is death*" (Romans 6:23); spiritual death is being spoken of here and the significance being "eternal separation"

> "And you He made alive, who were dead in trespasses and sins"
>
> (Ephesians 2:1)

Furthermore the apostle John tells us:

> "If anyone sees his brother sinning a sin which does not lead to death, he will ask, and He will give him life for those who commit sin not leading to death. There is sin leading to death. I do not say that he should pray about that. All unrighteousness is sin, and there is sin not leading to death." (1 John 5: 16-17)

Here is a reference to the "premature" demise of someone practicing sin, in order for them to escape the ultimate judgment of God and receive the recompense of eternal damnation; *"For whom the Lord loves He chastens, and scourges every son whom he receives ..."* (Hebrews 12: 6-8)

We find the word "**Sheol**" mentioned 65 times in the Old Testament, indicating this is the place set aside for those that die. The following are a few verses *(from: English Standard Version, ESV)* where this word is found:

> *"The LORD kills and brings to life; he brings down to Sheol and raises up."* (1 Samuel 2:6)

> *"Oh that you would hide me in Sheol, that you would conceal me until your wrath be past, that you would appoint me a set time, and remember me!"* (Job 14:13)

> *"If I hope for Sheol as my house, if I make my bed in darkness"* (Job 17:13)

> *"For you will not abandon my soul to Sheol, or let your holy one see corruption."* (Psalm 16:10)

> *"...the cords of Sheol entangled me; the snares of death confronted me."* (Psalm 18:5)

> *"O LORD, you have brought up my soul from Sheol; you restored me to life from among those who go down to the pit."* (Psalm 30:3)

> *"Let death steal over them; let them go down to Sheol alive; for evil is in their dwelling place and in their heart."* (Psalm 55:15)

> *¿ What man can live and never see death? Who can deliver his soul from the power of Sheol?"* (Psalm 89:48)

> *"Whatever your hand finds to do, do it with your might, for there is no work or thought or knowledge or wisdom in Sheol, to which you are going."* (Ecclesiastes 9:10)

> *"Your pomp is brought down to Sheol, the sound of your harps; maggots are laid as a bed beneath you, and worms are your covers. ... But you are brought down to Sheol, to the far reaches of the pit.."* (Isaiah 14: 11, 15)

Now the Lord Jesus explained that in "Sheol", there is more than one place where souls can be sent after they depart from their physical body. We read his words:

""There was a certain rich man who was clothed in purple and fine linen and fared sumptuously every day. But there was a certain beggar named Lazarus, full of sores, who was laid at his gate, desiring to be fed with the crumbs which fell from the rich man's table. Moreover the dogs came and licked his sores.

So it was that the beggar died, and was carried by the angels to **Abraham's bosom**. *The rich man also died and was buried. And being in torments in* **Hades**, *he lifted up his eyes and saw Abraham afar off, and Lazarus in his bosom.*

"Then he cried and said, 'Father Abraham, have mercy on me, and send Lazarus that he may dip the tip of his finger in water and cool my tongue; for I am tormented in this flame.' But Abraham said, 'Son, remember that in your lifetime you received your good things, and likewise Lazarus evil things; but now he is comforted and you are tormented.

And besides all this, between us and you there is a **great gulf** *fixed, so that those who want to pass from here to you cannot, nor can those from there pass to us.' "* (Luke 16: 19-26)

Believers who depart in the Lord are blessed and go directly to heaven:

"...having a desire to depart and be with Christ, which is far better." (Philippians 1:23)

"Here is the patience of the saints; here are those who keep the commandments of God and the faith of Jesus. Then I heard a voice from heaven saying to me, "Write: 'Blessed are the dead who die in the Lord from now on.' " "Yes," says the Spirit, "that they may rest from their labors, and their works follow them." (Revelation 14:12-13)

There are two places where others are sent, depending on their deeds (or what they neglected to do) while alive on the earth. One place is Hades and the other is Abraham's Bosom.

It Is Necessary To Elaborate A Little More On This Point

Addressing the question of Punishment

The Lord Jesus taught:

> *And that servant who knew his master's will, and did not prepare himself or do according to his will, shall be beaten with many stripes.*
>
> **But he who did not know,** *yet committed things deserving of stripes,* **shall be beaten with few.** *For everyone to whom much is given, from him much will be required; and to whom much has been committed, of him they will ask the more."* (Luke 12: 47-48)

He also said:

> *"For God did not send His Son into the world to condemn the world, but that the world through Him might be saved.*
> *"He who believes in Him is not condemned; but* **he who does not believe is condemned already,** *because he has not believed in the name of the only begotten Son of God.*
>
> *And this is the condemnation, that the light has come into the world, and men loved darkness rather than light, because their deeds were evil.*
>
> *For everyone practicing evil hates the light and does not come to the light, lest his deeds should be exposed."* (John 3: 17-20)

The Judgment Seat of Christ

I firmly believe the Bible shows us those who are Christians and have lived as believers *(accepted Jesus died on the cross for their sins)*, go directly to the **judgment seat of Christ**, and their works are weighed in the balance as we read in the following verses:

> *"Therefore we make it our aim, whether present or absent, to be well pleasing to Him. For we must all appear before the judgment seat of Christ, that each one may receive the things done in the body, according to what he has done, whether good or bad."*
> (2 Corinthians 5: 9-10)

The results of this judgment determine where the person is sent:

1. HEAVEN
2. ABRAHAMS' BOSOM, or;
3. HADES

It is said to those that go to HEAVEN:

" 'Come, you blessed of My Father, inherit the kingdom prepared for you from the foundation of the world"
(Matthew 25:34)

> *"'Well done, good and faithful servant; you were faithful over a few things, I will make you ruler over many things. Enter into the joy of your lord.'"*
> (Matthew 25:21)

A natural question may follow along these lines:

Where do those who receive few stripes go to while waiting for the final judgment day?

- If a person dies *without hearing the full truth* of the gospel of Jesus Christ, they did not have the opportunity to **reject or receive** the grace of God. They are sent to **Hades** after they die and there wait for the final judgment day, to be judged according to their works on earth.

- If a person put their faith in Christ Jesus, but due to ignorance or wrong teaching they committed acts that violated the moral law of God *(The 10 Commandments, Exodus 20; 3-17; Deuteronomy 5: 7-21)*; this individual is sent to **Abraham's Bosom**. The fact the person did not go directly to heaven after departing from the earth can be considered "**few stripes.**"

There is a real PLACE called Abraham's Bosom

To the best of my knowledge, I believe that the words of Jesus concerning "Abraham's Bosom refer an actual "**place**" and not merely a "state of being of the soul." I believe God has prepared this place for those whom will receive "few stripes" after appearing before the judgment seat of Christ. Those translated to paradise immediately will not be subjected to this.

The departed souls that go to ABRAHAM'S BOSOM **suffer the anguish of separation from God.** On the final judgment day they will be called by God, exonerated from condemnation and able to join the Lord in heaven:

> "For if we would judge ourselves, we would not be judged.
> But when we are judged, we are <u>chastened</u> by the Lord, *that we may not be condemned with the world.*" (1 Corinthians 11: 31-32)

The human soul has the natural inclination to desire the presence of its Creator, making any separation a painful "punishment" for the time spent apart. This is as if a good father finds it necessary to discipline his child for wrong actions. He may send the child away from his presence...though he certainly continues to love him and will restore him at the appropriate time.

> *"My soul thirsts for God, for the living God"* (Psalm 42:2)
>
> *"O God, You are my God... My soul thirsts for You"*
> (Psalm 63:1)
>
> *"My soul longs, yes, even faints For the courts of the LORD"* (Psalm 84:2)

Within the faithful covenant given to the descendants of King David were references to the manner God would deal with them:

> *"He shall cry to Me, 'You are my Father, My God, and the rock of my salvation.' Also I will make him My firstborn, The highest of the kings of the earth. My mercy I will keep for him forever, And My covenant shall stand firm with him.*
>
> *His seed also I will make to endure forever, And his throne as the days of heaven.*
>
> *"If his sons forsake My law And do not walk in My judgments, If they break My statutes And do not keep My commandments, Then I will punish their transgression with the rod, And their iniquity with stripes. Nevertheless My loving-kindness I will not utterly take from him, Nor allow My faithfulness to fail."*
> (Psalm 89: 26-33)

On the other hand, some who call themselves "believers" will be sent to **Hades** after appearing before the judgment seat of Christ. The Lord will tell them:

"'I never knew you; depart from Me, you who practice lawlessness!'" (Matthew 7:23)

"'Depart from me, you cursed, into the eternal fire prepared for the devil and his angels." (Matthew 25:41)

These will have their names erased from the Book of Life *(Revelation 3:5; 22:19);* and find no hope for them on Judgment Day. They will be tossed into the "Lake of Fire."

We should recall what is written:

"For if we go on sinning deliberately after receiving the knowledge of the truth, there no longer remains a sacrifice for sins, but a fearful expectation of judgment, and a fury of fire that will consume the adversaries.

Anyone who has set aside the law of Moses dies without mercy on the evidence of two or three witnesses. How much worse punishment, do you think, will be deserved by the one who has trampled underfoot the Son of God, and has profaned the blood of the covenant by which he was sanctified, and has outraged the Spirit of grace?

For we know him who said, "Vengeance is mine; I will repay." And again, "The Lord will judge his people." It is a fearful thing to fall into the hands of the living God." (Hebrews 10: 26-31)

The Bible says **every living soul** will **give account to God** at the Judgment:

The Bible states everyone who has ever been born shall be judged. Those with faith in the Lord Jesus will be judged by Him at the "Judgment Seat of Christ" *(2 Corinthians 5:10);* and everyone else will be judged according to their works and the **conviction of their conscience**, as Apostle Paul writes in his letter to the Romans:

"For God shows no partiality. All who have sinned without the law will also perish without the law, and all who have sinned under the law will be judged by the law.

For it is not the hearers of the law who are righteous before God, but the doers of the law who will be justified.

For when Gentiles, who do not have the law, by nature do what the law requires, they are a law to themselves, even though they do not have the law.

They show that the work of the law is written on their hearts, while their conscience also bears witness, and their conflicting thoughts **accuse or even excuse them** <u>on that day when</u>, *according to my gospel,* <u>God judges the secrets of men by Christ Jesus</u>*".*
(Romans 2: 11-16)

At the final Judgment Day all those in Hades will stand before the Great White Throne and those deemed unworthy to spend eternity in Heaven will be cast into the lake that burns with fire and brimstone. They will stay there for an eternity in torment with the devil and his angels.

"Then I saw a great white throne and Him who sat on it, from whose face the earth and the heaven fled away. And there was found no place for them.

And I saw the dead, small and great, standing before God, and books were opened. And another book was opened, which is the Book of Life. **And the dead were judged according to their works**, *by the things which* **were written** *in the books.*

The sea gave up the dead who were in it, and Death and Hades delivered up the dead who were in them. And they were judged, each one according to his works.

Then Death and Hades were cast into the lake of fire. This is the second death. And **anyone not found written** *in the Book of Life was cast into the lake of fire."* (Revelation 20: 11-15)

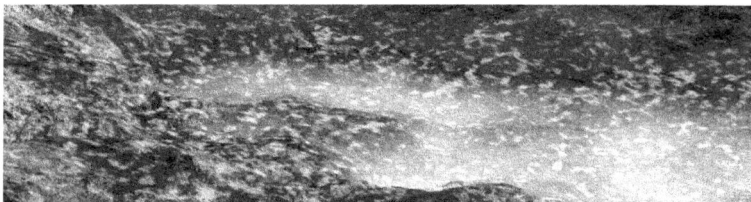

104

Where does all hope end?

When is all hope lost?

We'll go back to **the original question** formulated here at the beginning:

Is there any hope those who died have their name written in the Book of Life on the final Judgment Day, making it therefore possible to allow a Holy God give them entrance into Heaven for eternity?

Those educated in sound orthodox Christian doctrine must naturally respond NO, as anyone who dies without accepting Christ is already condemned by God to Hell, and will only appear at the final judgment to reaffirm this sentence and be cast into the Lake of Fire.

Nevertheless, the Bible tells us God is a JUST JUDGE. **At the judgment no one will be condemned** without proof they are guilty.

In the part of Seoul which is Hades will be people who rejected Christ, those who never had the opportunity to hear the good news of the gospel of salvation, and others who claimed to be "believers" during their lifetime but their testimony and actions demonstrated otherwise. In the other place, Abraham's Bosom, will be those who lived and believed Jesus is Lord but ignorantly offended God practicing religious rituals and traditions that are wrong and deceptive, though they were unaware of their malicious origin.

Can their names be written in the Book of Life on the final Day of Judgment?

Anyone who dies **without having put their faith in the Lord Jesus Christ** will go directly to **Hades**, and there wait for the last and final judgment. **It is among these** that, being **judged according to their works** and the conviction of their **consciences** *(Romans 2:11-16),* God either casting them into the lake of fire or writing their name in the Book of Life. Those written in the Book of Life will enter into heaven for eternity, having demonstrated mercy to others and able to obtain the same from God.

> *"For judgment is without mercy to the one who has shown no mercy. Mercy triumphs over judgment."* (James 2: 13)

In mentioning this last group, they **will not receive the rewards** given to faithful Christians when they come before the Lord.

With this we understand it to be possible to have ones name erased from the Book of Life *(Revelation 3:5, 22:19),* and also, **Yes** it is possible to have someone written into the Book of Life on the final judgment day

Let us remember the words of Christ:

> *"If I had not come and spoken to them, **they would have no sin**"*
> (John 15:22)

> *"Then some of the Pharisees who were with Him heard these words, and said to Him, "Are we blind also?"*
> *Jesus said to them, "If you were blind, **you would have no sin**; but now you say, 'We see.' Therefore your sin remains. "*
> *(John 9: 40-41)*

The Lord speaks to us of spiritual matters.

There is **spiritual blindness** and He relates this to being guilty of sin.

We should then answer the following question:

Will a Christian who commits sin enter heaven?

Many believers say that *"if we sin we cannot be saved".* Nevertheless, we consider that pride, jealousy, rivalries and bitterness are *"common failures";* although for God, those are works of the flesh. (See: Galatians 5: 19-21).

No one suggests that those who fall into these sins are lost; but the Bible says: *"...those who do such things will not inherit the kingdom of God."* (Galatians 5:21)

Even further, if it is insisted by some that God presently demands perfection in believers, then we pose the next question:

"Is a Christian rooted in Christ based on their righteousness, or is the righteousness of Christ attributed to them by faith?"

If a Christian is saved by living a life without sin, then salvation is no longer by grace, but by works!

Consequentially, if a believer is only accepted having no faults, then the Christian is not free from condemnation as insisted by Paul in Romans 8:1.

The believer then enter a continual exercise of fear followed by condemnation as we examine our soul; thus not entering into the joy of the knowledge that we are saved.

The Bible tells us:

> *"But God demonstrates His own love toward us, in that while we were still sinners, Christ died for us. Much more then, **having now been justified by His blood, we shall be saved from wrath through Him.***
>
> *For if when we were enemies we were reconciled to God through the death of His Son, **much more, having been reconciled, we shall be saved by His life...** "* (Romans 5: 8-11)

ALSO:

> *"For in that He Himself has suffered, being tempted, He is **able to aid** those who are tempted."* (Hebrews 2:18)

> *"Now to Him who is **able to keep you from stumbling**, And to present you faultless Before the presence of His glory with exceeding joy, To God our Savior, Who alone is wise, Be glory and majesty, Dominion and power, Both now and forever. Amen."* (Jude 24-25)

This Conviction Maintains Our Joy In Him.

But, as we also are conscious of **our existence in a depraved world,** we should be encouraged in knowing we can continually ask the Holy Spirit to **examine** our heart; and if He reveals unconfessed sin, we then must proceed to confess it and repent.

Remember the Lord Jesus, as He taught us to pray *(the Lord's Prayer),* tells us that every day, as well as asking for our daily bread, we should ask God to forgive us for all our trespasses.
The Lord Jesus is Faithful, always Faithful. **He will never abandon us** to the enemy at the end of our life.

The Bible says:

> *"God is faithful, who will not allow you to be tempted beyond what you are able, but with the temptation will also make the way of escape, that you may be able to bear it."* (1 Cor. 10:13)

> *"If we are faithless, He remains faithful; He cannot deny Himself."* (2 Timothy 2:13)

The Word also teaches us that those in *Christ "have crucified the flesh with its passions and desires"* and "**should walk in the SPIRIT"** (Galatians 5:24-25);

And in being lead by the Spirit of God we have the testimony that we are the **children of God** (Romans 8:14)

For that person who walks **in obedience** to God, being **sensitive** to the leading of the **Holy Spirit**, watching in order to keep from falling into the wiles of the Deceiver; **Working on the weak areas** the Spirit reveals exist and allowing Him to **mold** and transform them from glory to glory in the image of Christ Jesus every day (2 Cor. 3:18);

Putting aside their personal agenda and permitting **the will of God** to be done in their life (Psalm 138:8; Matthew 6:10; 26:39); they will grow and mature spiritually every day.

Such a person would **have learned** to defend themselves from the attacks and temptations, and would experience the victorious power of the cross in various manifestations as they walk with Christ; as also they will be able to say as did Apostle Paul:

"...it is no longer I who live, but Christ lives in me."
(Galatians 2:20)

And also:

"Who shall separate us from the love of Christ? Shall tribulation, or distress, or persecution, or famine, or nakedness, or peril, or sword?"

"Yet in all these things we are more than conquerors through Him who loved us.

For I am persuaded that neither death nor life, nor angels nor principalities nor powers, nor things present nor things to come, nor height nor depth, nor any other created thing, shall be able to separate us from the love of God which is in Christ Jesus our Lord." (Romans 8: 35, 37-39)

111

If, after being purified from past sins, someone is in sin **just before** the return of the Lord, or if they die before repenting of that sin or while in the act of sin, the consequence when he/she appear before the Lord **will depend** on the type of "Christian" life he/she lived.

If for example, the person has lived their life in the fear of God, kept their testimony and obeyed the instructions of the Holy Spirit, this person has the assurance of knowing that the weight of the works of obedience in their life is greater than the fall into their last sin, for which reason the Lord shall say:

> *"'Well done, good and faithful servant... Enter into the joy of your lord.'"*   (Mathew 25:21)

Because our PERFECTION **is not measured by how few times we have fallen into sin**, as we have seen the Bible declare: *" if we say we have no sin, we deceive our own selves"* (1 John 1:8);

But **how we walk in obedience** to God and His Word, permitting the Holy Spirit to conclude His work of perfecting us.

We see this graphically:

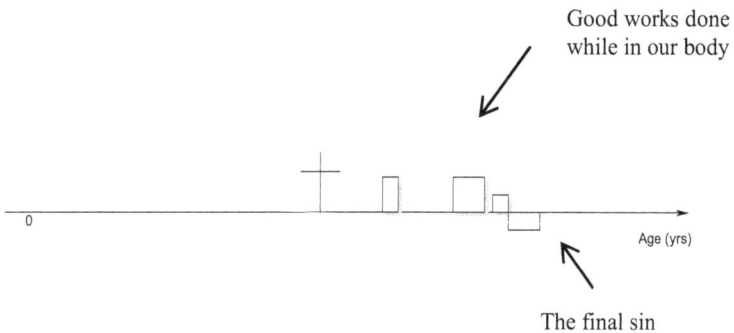

Good works done while in our body

Age (yrs)

The final sin

Nevertheless, this gives us no cause to abuse the grace of God, as the Bible strongly emphasizes:

> *"For if we sin willfully after we have received the knowledge of the truth,* there no longer remains a sacrifice for sins,
> but a certain *fearful expectation of judgment,* and fiery indignation which will devour the adversaries.
>
> Anyone who has rejected Moses' law dies without mercy on the testimony of two or three witnesses.
>
> *Of how much worse punishment,* do you suppose, will he be thought worthy who has trampled the Son of God underfoot, counted the blood of the covenant by which he was sanctified a common thing, and insulted the Spirit of grace?"
>
> (Hebrews 10: 26-29)

To "sin willingly" is the same as "rebellion".

That being so, if a person continually sins, after being purified of past sins, the weight of those sins is once again borne by their soul…

…Y And if he/she dies in that condition and comes before the tribunal of Christ to be judged, if the weight of his/her sins is greater than the good works done, he/she **can be rejected.**

It can be illustrated like this:

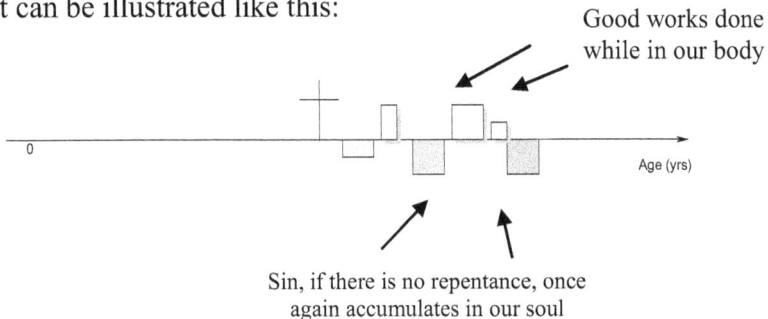

Good works done while in our body

0

Age (yrs)

Sin, if there is no repentance, once again accumulates in our soul

IN RELATION TO THIS, THE BIBLE SAYS:

> *"**Do not be deceived, God is not mocked**; for whatever a man sows, that he will also reap. For he who sows to his flesh will of the flesh reap corruption, but he who sows to the Spirit will of the Spirit reap everlasting life."* (Galatians 6: 7-8)

> *"For we must ALL appear before **the judgment seat of Christ**, that each one may receive the things done in the body, according to what he has done, **whether good or bad.**"* (2 Cor. 5:10)

> *"And now, little children, abide in Him, that when He appears, we may have confidence **and not be ashamed before Him at His coming.**"* (1 John 2:28)

> *"Blessed are those **who wash their robes, so that they may have the right to the tree of life** and that they may enter the city by the gates"* (Revelation 22:14, ESV)

> *"**He who overcomes** shall be clothed in white garments, and I **will not blot out his name** from the Book of Life; but I will confess his name before My Father and before His angels."* (Revelation 3:5)

THE BIBLE ALSO SAYS:

> *"**Not everyone who says to Me, 'Lord, Lord,'** shall enter the kingdom of heaven, but he who **DOES** the will of My Father in heaven.*
>
> *Many will say to Me in that day, 'Lord, Lord, have we not prophesied in Your name, cast out demons in Your name, and done many wonders in Your name?' And then I will declare to them, 'I never knew you; **depart from Me, you who practice lawlessness!'*** (Mathew 7: 21-23)

> *"The LORD is slow to anger and great in power, And **will not at all acquit the wicked.**"* (Nahum 1:3, NKJV)

> *"The LORD is slow to anger and great in power, and the LORD **will by no means clear the guilty.**"* (Nahum 1:3, ESV)

*"But why do you judge your brother? Or why do you show contempt for your brother? For **we shall all stand before the judgment seat of Christ.** For it is written: "AS I LIVE, SAYS THE LORD, EVERY KNEE SHALL BOW TO ME, AND EVERY TONGUE SHALL CONFESS TO GOD." So **then each of us shall give account of himself to God.**"*
(Romans 14:10-12)

So, this is **more serious** than we may realize at first glance.

Moreover: Concerning those that are believers for a season, and then **abandon** the way of the Lord, the Bible tells us that their situation is worse than before they became believers:

*"For if, after they have escaped the pollutions of the world through the knowledge of the Lord and Savior Jesus Christ, **they are again entangled in them** and overcome, **the latter end is worse for them than the beginning.***

*For **it would have been better for them** not to have known the way of righteousness, than having known it, to turn from the holy commandment delivered to them."*   (2 Peter 2: 20-21)

We now reiterate, God cannot be mocked.

We should live conforming to the Word that assures us **a true Christian is not in a revolving door, entering and leaving the grace of God**; but is sure in the hands of God, now that:

*"...neither death nor life, nor angels nor principalities nor powers, nor things present nor things to come, nor height nor depth, nor any other created thing, shall be able to separate us from **the love of God** which is in Christ Jesus our Lord."*
(Romans 8: 38-39)

115

A sinful life is unnatural for the true Christian

We may even call it "anti- natural". We can no longer commit the same old sins. Having been born of the Spirit, a believer is a new creature for which "*old things have passed and all things have become new*" (2 Cor. 5:17).

Our old life is past; **and though its dormant force may remain**, it is dominated and declared dead **by the new Presence** that abides in us (Romans 6:11).

That which before was a practice and habit, has now changed and becomes unnatural, and contrary to the new desires of our heart.

As the apostle John says:

> *"Whoever abides in Him does not sin. Whoever sins has neither seen Him nor known Him. Little children, let no one deceive you. He who practices righteousness is righteous, just as He is righteous.*
>
> *He who sins is of the devil, for the devil has sinned from the beginning. For this purpose the Son of God was manifested, that He might destroy the works of the devil.*
>
> *Whoever has been born of God does not sin, for His seed remains in him; and he cannot sin, because he has been born of God."*
> (1 John 3: 6-9)

> *"We know that everyone who has been born of God does not keep on sinning, but he who was born of God protects him, and the evil one does not touch him."* (1 John 5:18, ESV)

Expressed in another way, sin is alien to our new nature as the new creature in Christ through faith DOES NOT **practice sin.**

Who is in Control now?

Who Is in Control Now?

Now, when the old nature regains control, temporarily and unexpectedly, our new man opposes this unnatural intrusion. We immediately turn to Christ

The Bible tells us that though we be unfaithful to the Lord, He remains always faithful.

He cannot deny himself (2 Timothy 2:13)

The Lord is always there to intercede on our behalf before the Father *(Hebrews 7:25),* demonstrating his love for us will never fail.

When the believer who has sinned returns to Christ, he does not come with the desperation of a lost soul, but in full understanding that **as he is a child of God**, he has an Advocate with the Father, who is Faithful and Just, and will forgive our sin and cleanse us of all shame.

This is how the believer exercises his prerogative as a child of God, **without doubting his position** based on the knowledge of the infallible righteousness of Christ by faith.

Nevertheless, it is necessary to show the correlation between free will and our responsibility as believers, as God NEVER REMOVES **the ability to choose freely** when He receives us as his son/ daughter.

By the exercise of free will, the believer accepts salvation, and becomes a child of God; but should also be cautious and **not have a careless attitude toward sin**.

He cannot apply the grace of God as a license to sin.

The Word teaches that our God,
As He is **LOVE** *(1 John 4:16),*
Is also a **CONSUMING FIRE** *(Deut. 4:24)*

What shall we say then? Shall we continue in sin so that grace may abound? Paul asked *(Romans 6:1)*

Certainly not!, was the answer (Romans 6:2).

The answer is an EMPHATIC NO! Paul knew and taught that to practice sin adversely affects the faith of a believer; and faith is what makes our fellowship with God possible.

It is presumptuous, arbitrary, and an evidence of rebellion to continue in sin. To rebel is contrary to obedience demonstrated through faith.

Believers should be constantly vigilant:

> *"**Looking carefully** lest anyone fall short of the grace of God; lest any root of bitterness springing up cause trouble, and by this many become defiled"* (Hebrews 12:15)

The exhortation of the Bible is:

> *"**Examine** yourselves as to whether you are in the faith. **Test** yourselves"* (2 Corinthians 13:5)

Because:

*"Blessed is the man who remains steadfast under trial, for when he has stood the test **he will receive the crown of life**, which God has promised to those who love him."* (James 1:12)

Jesus tells us:

"Behold, I am coming soon, bringing my recompense with me, TO REPAY each one for what he has done" (Rev. 22:12, ESV)

A final word:

Let us live our life in a manner that enables us to appropriate the words of the Apostle Paul:

"Do you not know that those who run in a race all run, but one receives the prize? Run in such a way that you may obtain it.
And everyone who competes for the prize is temperate in all things. Now they do it to obtain a perishable crown, but we for an imperishable crown.
Therefore I run thus: not with uncertainty. Thus I fight: not as one who beats the air. But I discipline my body and bring it into subjection, lest, when I have preached to others, I myself should become disqualified." (1 Corinthians 9: 24-27)

*"I have fought the good fight, I have finished the race, I have kept the faith. Finally, **there is laid up for me the crown of righteousness**, which the Lord, the righteous Judge, will give to me on that Day, and not to me only but also to all who have loved His appearing."*
(2 Timothy 4: 7-8)

We should live in the Truth and teach others only the Truth. We trust in God always, as He will never fail us.

"To him who overcomes I will grant to sit with Me on My throne, as I also overcame and sat down with My Father on His throne.
He who has an ear, let him hear what the Spirit says to the churches" (Revelation 3: 21-22)

Blessings and Peace!

121

From atheist to Pastor.

A personal anecdote

From atheist to Pastor. A personal anecdote

As of the moment I am writing these lines I've passed the important age of fifty years old. After being taught the traditional Christian religion, I became an atheist in 1974, while in my sophomore year at the university. After studies in philosophy; and being exposed to the depth of thought of the great philosophers; I accepted their teachings. I also perceived how there were very many contradictions even amongst them.

My mother, father, and a brother were Christians. I would mock them, argue vehemently with them, and spoke disparagingly of the pastor that would visit them, as I thought he was a deceiver. I hated to even hear the word "God." Anger would flow through me when I heard that word. As I read and studied, if the author mentioned the word "God", I would immediately discard and even toss the book, considering it to be "junk."

I now remember as a child that whenever I would sneeze, my mother would say "God Bless You." Well, in those days I would ask my mother to stop saying those words to me as I had disdain for the word "God."

I told my mother that since sneezing was the sign that my body was receptive to germs, she should say "Health" instead.

She departed to be with the Lord in 1978, three weeks after attending my graduation; with the pain of knowing her son was rebellious and she could not utter a blessing for him *(But I could never stop her from praying for me when she had devotions; and I am sure God heard her prayers and in His time answered them)*.

I graduated as a Chemical Engineer in June 1978 and worked in my profession. I was able to develop and expanded the acquired knowledge in my specialty as an employee of all the companies that hired me.

Since I didn't believe in God, I had evolutionary beliefs, and sought in all science the answers to the questions my heart demanded.

I had a particular definition of what God was. I believed:

> "God was a myth created by feeble and ignorant minds that had as a purpose, other than motivating people to become good citizens; comforting poor souls for their lack of competence or intellect. This vain illusion would compensate them for the failure in their lives, as after death they would live well."

For a long time, I sought to discover why things exist or occur as they do; for example, how is it the light and brightness of the sun continues for so many years without diminishing? Why does the force of gravity exist, is the universe without limits, or what causes the perfection of the atom, etc?

Who was the designer of that computer?

I would imagine the possibility of the existence of an advanced **computer** somewhere in the universe that controlled everything and designed gravity to stop the stars from colliding. Then the question would arise:

Who designed and programmed that computer?
Where was the mind behind such perfection in the universe?

I had so many questions and science was not satisfying my troubled mind (although I was then a technical consultant with my field of expertise being scientific and technical information; responsible for answering all the inquiries from professionals in all fields.)

In 1988, my older brother asked me if I had anyone I could consider as a best friend. I told him I had friends, but in the final analysis, I trusted no one. I considered myself alone.

He invited me to a meeting where he would introduce me to someone that could be my best friend, and I would truly be able to trust.

I went to the meeting and saw it was held in a Catholic church where the catechism group and charismatic believers among them were presenting Jesus Christ. I became somewhat frustrated with my brother, but remained there with him. The following Saturday the presentation would continue.

Many things occurred in my life during the next week and I was in anguish. When I opened the Bible I saw passages that spoke of judgment and destruction, but also other verses that spoke of God's desire to forgive me, that He loved me, etc.

I returned to the next meeting and felt more tranquil, although awaiting something. I continued attending the Catholic Church though I was ashamed to tell my neighbors and friends I now believed in God and Jesus Christ truly existed.

I immigrated to the United States in April 1990 intent on starting a consulting and importing business, which would make me a millionaire; but God had a different plan for my life.

Although I wanted nothing to do with other Christian sects *(I called them Protestants in a demeaning manner or more cordially, our "separated brethren")* in August of that year the Lord brought me to "New Life Fellowship" church and in December of that year I participated in water baptism.

I started serving Him, willing to allow His purpose to be fulfilled in me. The Lord has showed much to me and I am sure more will follow. I know I am in his hands, and I ask His perfect will be done in my life.

J.R.

I invite you to know

Love *as a Person*

The Manifestation of Love

There is a force that moves all humanity. It is more powerful than electricity, conquers more than does money, and has a stronger pull than gravity.

This is the force of Love

It emanates from the source of all things created: GOD. His Word tells us that GOD wants to demonstrate HIS love to every person. This includes YOU. He tells you:

> *"I drew you with cords of a man, with bands of love"*
> Hosea 11:4

These cords speak of a sacrifice, thru love, that made it possible to save YOU.

Maybe your ways are far from God, nevertheless, He seeks you to save you, bless you, prosper you, and above all have fellowship with you.

> *"For God so loved the world that He gave His only begotten Son, that whoever believes in Him should not perish but have everlasting life"* (John 3:16)

> *"But God demonstrates His own love toward us, in that while we were still sinners, Christ died for us."* (Romans 5:8)

Draw near to God. He is your Creator. Allow Him to save you. Do not resist the call of His love.

It is very easy to receive the forgiveness of God, as Christ paid the price that was demanded.

Do your part now:

Make the decision today to change your life. Repent of having lived outside the will of God, your Creator, whom one day you will have to give account for all your actions and words *(Matthew 12:36; Ecclesiastes 12: 13-14)*; and accept the justice and grace of God in Jesus Christ now, before you no longer have any more opportunities:

a) Recognize you are a sinner. You have not been perfect before God.

b) Repent for being away from God.

c) Ask for forgiveness with all your heart for all your transgressions.

d) Give your soul and the control of your life to God, confessing Jesus Christ as your Lord and Savior; and receive the grace of God, the salvation of your soul.

The Lord says:

> *"Come now, and let us reason together, Says the LORD, Though your sins are like scarlet, They shall be as white as snow; Though they are red like crimson, They shall be as wool."* *(Isaiah 1: 18)*

> *"That if you confess with your mouth the Lord Jesus and believe in your heart that God has raised Him from the dead, you will be saved."* (Romans10:9)

> *"If we confess our sins, He is faithful and just to forgive us our sins and to cleanse us from all unrighteousness."* *(1 John 1:9)*

> *"and the blood of Jesus Christ His Son cleanses us from all sin"* *(1 John 1:7b)*

e) Learn to live in God's will. To accomplish this, it is necessary to speak with Him (pray); Learn what God desires for you *(read the Bible)* and attend a local church where the Word of God, the Bible, is preached and taught, so you may grow in the knowledge of the Word of God and in brotherly love; and obey the voice of the Holy Spirit Who will guide you all the time.

f) Share the love you have received from God with others.

Blessings.

Additional Books written by the Author

Additional Books written by the Author

The Paradigm, or Tale? of Evolution

The author is a former atheist who believed in and adamantly defended the Theory of Evolution for 14 years during and after his studies at the Pontifical Catholic University 'Madre y Maestra' in Santiago, D.R.

The Paradigm, or Tale?

of Evolution

A Christian-Scientific Research

2nd Edition

Julio A. Rodriguez

He graduated as a Chemical Engineer in 1978; and as a result of 30 years of intense investigations on evolutionary theory, and innumerable life experiences he shares his conclusions.

This book details "evolutionary" thought with such impact to make you seriously question:

- Was all that exists; made by "Someone" or "Nothing"?
- Was there a Wise Being, Powerful and Eternal, who made all things; or did all begin out of "Nothingness" which never existed and never had power, a purpose...nothing at all!, formed the complete universe with its essence of nothing?
- Life? Is there a purpose or sense, or a vain illusion we must all tolerate?

The author asserts and demonstrates:

" Our schools and universities indoctrinate students against a belief in God, teaching as scientific fact purely atheistic-religiosity", and also: "If someone were to believe the universe was formed by a particle smaller than an atom, this person would **have more faith** than someone who professes faith in God"

Religious Gladiators. Beware of Contemporary Judaizers

The main theme of this book is of extreme importance for Christian believers today.

There is a subtle attempt by false teachers to enter churches and lead astray the faithful, under the guise of teaching Jewish culture.

In many instances they have confused brethren lacking a solid foundation and as a consequence some have **unwittingly rejected the grace of God** manifested thru Jesus Christ; seeking justification thru the works of the law.

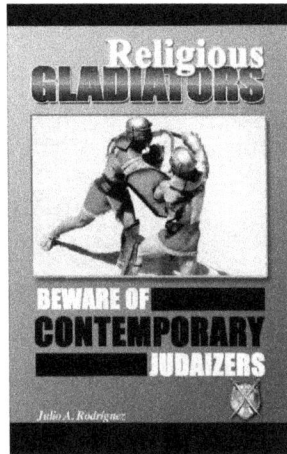

ATHEISM HAS No Foundation

An investigative compilation of ideas and scientific - philosophical concepts, exposing the myths and dogmas of scientific atheists

"Without mattering what a person believes or understands about his/her own existence, logic and reason within them disturbs and compels them to look for answers for the purpose of life; because it is obvious that their life is slowing passing by.

In this book, wise expressions of God-believing great scientists are presented; in contrast to the improbable myths that Atheistic Scientists declare.

Due to the fact that the basic questions of life do not have satisfactory answers in Atheism, those that call themselves "Atheists" have resorted to the absurd rejection of verified facts, promoting fables disguised as scientific truths; and making pretentious unfounded declarations, attempting to calm and silence the conscience of everyone who asks a reason why they believe what they believe"

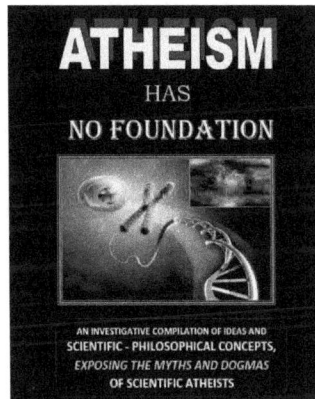

IS A POWERFUL TOOL FOR EVERY BELIEVER; CHALLENGE AND A KEY TO ALL THOSE WHO SEEK TO KNOW ABSOLUTE TRUTH.

References

[i] **New King James Version (NKJV)** The Holy Bible, New King James Version Copyright © 1982 by Thomas Nelson, Inc.

King James Version (KJV) by Public Domain

English Standard Version (ESV) The Holy Bible, English Standard Version Copyright © 2001 by Crossway Bibles, a division of Good News Publishers.

American Standard Version (ASV) Copyright © 1901 by Public Domain

[ii] Summary of Christian Doctrine, by Luis Berkhof, pg. 76

[iii] The five points of Calvinism, by Edwin H. Palmer, p. 122

[iv] Confession of Augsburg, Article 2.

[v] Source: Philip SCAF. The History of Christian Church, Vol II P 246

[vi] Source: ISBE, 1979

[vii] Source: Britannica 1979 VII, Page 837-8

[viii] Source: Westminster confession of faith

www.ingramcontent.com/pod-product-compliance
Lightning Source LLC
Chambersburg PA
CBHW061734020426
42331CB00006B/1237